INTO A NEW WORLD

INTO A NEW WORLD

Dieter Hain

TEACH Services, Inc.
www.TEACHServices.com

Copyright © 2009 Dieter Hain and TEACH Services, Inc.
ISBN-13: 978-1-57258-582-9
Library of Congress Control Number: 2009921343

Published by

TEACH Services, Inc.
www.TEACHServices.com

Table of Contents

Introduction	Into a New World	7
Chapter 1	Reflection On The Paris Youth Congress	9
Chapter 2	Fiery Trails	12
Chapter 3	Surprise at Langenbach	19
Chapter 4	A Test of Faith	23
Chapter 5	Marienhoehe	25
Chapter 6	Fire in The Dorm	31
Chapter 7	Bible Studies	34
Chapter 8	Good-bye Germany!	40
Chapter 9	Unexpected Delay	45
Chapter 10	Canada – Here I Come!	50
Chapter 11	Canadian Union College (CUC)	53
Chapter 12	More Canvassing	61
Chapter 13	Back on Campus	66
Chapter 14	Working Vacations	68
Chapter 15	Mutti Joins Me!	71
Chapter 16	Parish Ministry	74
Chapter 17	Chaplaincy	79
Chapter 18	We Move To California	82
Chapter 19	Five Days to Freedom	97
Chapter 20	Walla Walla And Beyond	111
Chapter 21	We Move Again	118
Chapter 22	Epilogue	122
	Postscript	124

Dedication

To all who have found refuge in North America after being uprooted from their native lands, and who have decided to follow Jesus Christ.

Introduction

INTO A NEW WORLD

It was late into the evening on August 15, 1953. The monotonous drone of the propeller-driven airliner's four engines should have put me to sleep like it had my two American seatmates. For them, flying was routine. But for me, it was an exciting first. I couldn't relax.

Only two days before I had boarded a commercial plane in Frankfurt, Germany, bound for Paris, France. After an unforeseen delay in France due to an airline strike, I was now crossing the Atlantic Ocean heading for Montreal, Canada, bound for a New World!

To appreciate fully my excitement, you will need to read "ESCAPE," by Sandy Zaugg, published by Pacific Press in 2007. It is a story of my experiences as a German refugee in the latter part of World War II and the events following. Here is a brief summary.

Narrowly escaping the rapid advance of the Russian Army and a bombed-out railroad car, my mother and I relocated in Wallenfels, a small town in Bavaria.

When the Americans occupied the town, they treated us well and gave us food. In return for their kindness, I offered them my services since I had studied English in school. For almost three years I worked for the U.S. Army, first as custodian, then as interpreter on border patrols, and finally as company clerk. I loved it!

Returning to Wallenfels while the soldiers were on field maneuvers, I discovered that my mother was studying the Bible with some Adventists. She introduced me to Hans Zuber, a former non-commissioned officer in the German *Wehrmacht*. To my amazement, he was able to answer a question I had often pondered, "Why did Germany lose the War?" He did it using his Bible. This convinced me of the relevancy of that Book in our time. I decided to study for the ministry.

What follows is intended to fill in some blanks. Since the publication of "ESCAPE," people have asked for a more detailed account of my student years in Germany and why I decided to come to Canada rather then straight to the United States. Others want to know how I financed my education. Still others wondered how I could be a minister without being married. How did I meet the love of my life when we both had been engaged to other people?

If these questions and others trigger your interest, keep reading.

Chapter
1

REFLECTION ON THE PARIS YOUTH CONGRESS

As delegate from the small company of believers in Klein-Vichtach, I was among the more than 5,000 young people attending the 1951 Paris, France, Youth Congress. I had joined the Adventist church two and a half years earlier. Now I was eager to mingle with and observe other young people from all over Europe who shared my faith.

Many of those attending were citizens of countries who had fought each other during World War II. *How would we all get along?* I was not the only one who had such concerns. The Paris police, learning that 1,200 Germans were *invading* the exhibition grounds, were put on high alert. They were informed that representatives from across Europe, the USA, Africa, and even the USSR would be present. However, when nothing out of the ordinary happened for two days, their fears lessened considerably. By the third day, most of them had been called away, leaving only a skeleton crew near the entrance to the exhibition grounds.

The Congress began on Tuesday, July 24 and concluded the following Sunday afternoon. Except for Friday afternoon when the delegates were shown the sights of Paris and Versailles, meetings filled the rest of the time. There were devotionals, seminars, preaching services, and evening meetings when young people representing 25 countries shared methods in winning others to Christ.

During meal times we mingled freely with the youth from other nations. I met and formed a long-lasting friendship with a colporteur from Northern Ireland and spoke to students from La Sierra and Pacific Union College in California. This exposure galvanized my determination to study in America someday.

Early Sunday afternoon, delegates were organized into sections according to country and marched through the vast exhibition grounds, most in their colorful national costumes. Afterwards they posed for pictures. I had my picture taken with three young ladies from Algiers. They were dressed in flowing white robes with their faces covered except for their eyes. Some of the most colorful costumes were worn by Scandinavian and Southern European young people.

The press was on hand and pictures of the parade were published in the largest Paris newspapers. The most conservative, *France-Soir*, printed a special Youth Congress edition on that final Sunday. Our own Adventist *Youth Instructor* covered the event and filled half of their September 18, 1951, edition with stories and pictures. Here is a quote from this publication.

> "The Paris Youth's Congress had ended, but there was one last gesture of love and fellowship when the buses came to take the more than 1,200 German delegates to the railroad

station. There they would board their special train. Everyone still on the grounds came to say good-by. There were few dry eyes as these young Seventh-day Adventists headed back toward the country of stress and storm which is their homeland. Handkerchiefs damp though they were, waved wildly, and hands and coats and scarves waved too. The French dwellers in the across-the-street apartments joined in the farewell, waving towels, pillowcases, and even bedsheets!

The next morning, Pastor Aitken was leading a group in cleaning up the buildings and grounds. The Chief of Park Police approached him and asked, 'Monsieur Aitken, I have a boy, 14-years-old, and I want him to be a Missionary Volunteer. Tell me what must he do to join your organization? I have seen many demonstrations in this park, but I never have seen one like this. I did not know there were so many young people in the world who do not smoke or drink, who are good Christians like these. I want my boy to be one of them.'"

It had taken just six days for the residents of Paris to drop their prejudice. The love of Christ that reaches across all barriers had conquered once again. As we made our way home, singing our favorite hymns, we prayed that these French people would open their hearts to the one who made us so happy – our Savior, Lord, and Friend.

Chapter
2

FIERY TRIALS

A little over a year following my baptism, while attending Sabbath services in Klein-Vichtach, the presiding elder, Heinrich Igler, announced that Malchen Zuber, wife of Hans, my spiritual mentor, had been seriously hurt and was a patient in the Kronach hospital, lingering between life and death. He solicited the prayers of the congregation and support for Hans, who spent much of his time near his wife.

At the time the Zubers lived in the village of Unterrodach, halfway between Kronach and Klein-Vichtach. They occupied the second floor of a suburban residence. Malchen was in her mid fifties, moderately obese and of medium height. She was a frugal woman who knew how to save a penny. She had been canning pears and was alone at home when daylight faded. Used to turning off the lights when they weren't needed, she pulled her chair next to the stove. As the pot containing the canning jars slowly heated up, the surrounding warmth caused her to doze off.

When the water reached the boiling point, it began spilling over, making a hissing sound. Only half awake, she pulled the big pot toward her, intending to stop at the edge. Instead, it tipped over, emptying the entire contents over her lower body and legs.

In excruciating pain she screamed for help. The people living downstairs rushed to her side in time to prevent her from tearing at her skin. A doctor was called immediately, and ordered her transferred to the Kronach hospital.

For several weeks her recovery was in question. However, due to general good health, the loving care of her husband, and the prayers of her church family, she slowly gained ground. A year later she came back to church.

Her first appearance at church was a memorable one. She had often read 1 Peter 4:19, "So then, those who suffer according to God's will should . . . continue to do good." An accomplished organist with a beautiful soprano voice, she presented special music prior to the sermon. Accompanying herself on the old pump organ in Igler's living room where the congregation had assembled, she chose to sing, *Now Thank We All Our God.* We all joined her on the last stanza, many of us moved to tears. Her recovery was a miracle.

This was not the first time God had intervened in the life of the Zuber family. Her escape from a doomed air-raid shelter in the summer of 1943 also borders on the miraculous.

She and her two daughters, Ruth (21) and Martha (16), lived in the city of Hamburg, the largest seaport on the continent of Europe. Because of its naval shipyards and submarine base, Hamburg became a prime target for Allied air raids. During July and August of that year, approximately 50,000 people perished and half of the city's buildings were destroyed. Malchen and her daughters were used to being awakened in the middle of the night by the mournful wail of sirens. They would dress quickly and seek refuge in the basement of the apartment block where they lived. Hans was far away serving in the military.

It was almost midnight on July 27, 1943, when once again they were huddled together with others in the shelter. They had been spared direct hits in the past and were hoping for another reprieve. As the explosions came closer, the ground shook and the smoke began seeping through cracks of the shelter door. Apparently, their city block had been hit. Shortly after midnight the order to evacuate came. Forming a single line, they pushed open the door and felt the searing heat. A wall of fire surrounded them shooting skyward, devouring everything in its path. The Allies were using incendiary devices which sprayed phosphorous-like rain from the skies and kept burning, even in water. Breathing became difficult.

Turning around, Malchen pushed her daughters back toward their shelter. "Stay in here or you'll all be burned alive," she screamed to those trying to escape.

"We're getting out of here," others yelled as they forged on and later perished.

Some heeded Malchen's cry and returned to the shelter, joining her in search of water. Their own supply was used up. A narrow walkway connected all the shelters underneath their apartment block. Fortunately, they found one not far away with water stored in a large tub, surrounded by a small group of frightened people. Malchen discovered two gas masks and gave them to her daughters while she dipped a scarf into the water and wrapped it around her face. This helped some, but their situation was getting desperate.

"We must pray or perish," she shouted above the noise. Quoting Psalm 50:15, she continued: "Dear God, we claim your promise that those who call upon You in the day of trouble, will be delivered." Coughing, she continued, "Please Lord, fulfill this promise to us today!"

In silence, they waited for deliverance, trying to conserve oxygen. In the early morning hours they suddenly heard a commotion on the street above. "HELP! HELP! HELP!" they shouted in unison trying to attract attention to their plight. A Civil Defense official looking for his missing family heard them and immediately organized a rescue team. Successful in breaking through the concrete barrier that guarded the only shelter window, the rescuers created a hole large enough to pull everyone out.

Moments later they heard a big crash as dust billowed from the escape hole. The ceiling had collapsed. Malchen and her girls looked at each other in awe – their lives had been miraculously spared.

As the Civil Defense official led them to the school, the only building still standing in their neighborhood, Malchen pulled her girls close and whispered, "God has delivered us!" Tears of gratitude streaked down their dusty faces when they arrived at the school, which had been transformed into the First Aid station. By mid-morning a truck, which was provided by the Government, transported them and other survivors into the country for resettlement.

★ ★ ★

Meanwhile, Hans learned about the continuous bombardment of Hamburg and became alarmed. At the time, he was a Staff Sergeant in the German Army, stationed in Austria. He approached his commanding officer.

"Sir?"

"Yes, Sergeant." The commander continued looking over some papers on his desk.

"Sir, Hamburg has been bombed almost constantly for weeks now. My wife and two daughters live there. Would you grant me a short leave so I can search for them? All telephone connections are disrupted."

The commander was sympathetic. "Wait here Sergeant." He made a few phone calls, "I'll give you a long weekend leave. Good luck. But hurry back!"

"Thank you, sir." As he left, Hans breathed a prayer of thanks and added, "Dear Lord, help me find my family."

Arriving in Hamburg, he was not prepared for what he saw. The scene that unfolded before his eyes was indescribable. Smoldering ruins everywhere. Nothing looked familiar. "How could anyone have survived this?," he wondered. Finally, he discovered the area where they had lived. The entire apartment block was gone. As he trudged through the rubble, his every step was a silent prayer. "Dear God, please help me find my wife and daughters. I can't bear the thought of going on without them."

While looking for some familiar landmarks, he noticed another man, Fritz, an elderly neighbor who was also looking for family. Fritz glanced up only briefly and said, "Your family is safe. I saw them at the school. You are fortunate."

"Really Fritz, are you sure?" Excitement of the news gave him new energy.

"Yes, Hans. I talked with your wife. She and the girls were all right. Go on over to the school, they may still be there. All able survivors are being transported to the country before the next raid begins."

An enormous weight now lifted from Hans' shoulders as he rushed to the school. There he learned that his wife and daughters had departed for the country. Though they didn't see each other that day, Hans returned to his unit, assured that his loved ones were safe. God had heard his prayers.

* * *

Shortly before World War II ended, Hans was taken prisoner along with the rest of his unit. They were forced to walk from Austria to Belgrade, Yogoslavia, a distance of about 250 miles. They were given very little food and water, yet expected to cover a certain number of miles each day. Many fainted. The guards were under orders to finish them off and leave the bodies beside the road. Later this became known as the *Death March*, because so many German prisoners died. When they had marched about half-way, Hans, too began to feel weak and realized that he might not make it to Belgrade.

One night, while looking up into the stars from the barren field where the prisoners were camped, he prayed, "Dear Lord, please send me some nourishment so that I can go on. Without Your help, I'm done."

Sleep never came as he continued praying through the night. Early the next morning they marched on, shuffling along a gravel road silently, each man consumed with their own thoughts. Suddenly, Hans spotted the heel of a loaf of bread lying on the ground directly in front of him. Too weak to pick it up, he turned to his comrades.

"Did any of you lose a piece of bread?"

When no one answered, he asked the soldier marching beside him to retrieve it. Biting off a tiny piece, he tried chewing—but his mouth was too dry. Eventually, enough saliva formed to allow swallowing one small piece at a time. When the last morsel had vanished, he felt new energy pulsating through his body. Once again, God had intervened. He made it to Belgrade. After Armistice Day he was released, returned to Germany, and was eventually re-united with his wife and daughters.

Chapter
3

SURPRISE AT LANGENBACH

Once I was convinced of God's claim on my life, I decided not to return to my job with the United States Army. Instead, I planned to prepare for the ministry, but that would take money. For a short time I found employment in the nearby town of Zeyern with a kitchenware merchant. However, when I requested Sabbath privileges, he terminated me. However, God had a better plan. Hans Zuber's father-in-law was a sales representative for a well-known soap factory, and traveled house-to-house in a district too large for him to handle alone. He arranged for me to take half of his territory and spent some time training me. Soon I was knocking on doors, traveling on my trusted bicycle, and depending on the Lord to help me earn the needed funds to attend Seminary.

While selling soap products from house-to-house, I employed local residents to deliver the ordered merchandise and collect the money. Since the assigned areas had been worked previously, names of people who had functioned in that capacity were familiar. Langenbach, however, was *virgin territory*, and I had determined to win new customers.

Located six miles south of the Iron Curtain that separated East and West Germany, Langenbach was home to about 200 people, mostly farmers. The long, harsh winters and rainy summers made for brief growing seasons, depressing the local economy. I soon learned that the people hung on to their hard-earned money, buying only those goods they considered essential.

Still, I sold my products to several households and began my search for a *delivery person*. Again and again the name of *Goller* surfaced. The Gollers were elderly but honest and friendly folk. People urged me to visit them. So halfway through one afternoon, I knocked on their front door.

Their home was a typical farmhouse located in the center of town along the main thoroughfare, with three floors above ground and animal shelters under the same roof. The pungent smell of cow manure and a friendly lady greeted me. She introduced herself as Frau Goller. A broad hallway separated the stable from the residential area. While Frau Goller escorted me to their dining room, I noticed another lady working at the kitchen stove. Everything was meticulously clean, and there was no animal odor in this part of the home.

"This is my younger sister, Liesbet," Frau Goller explained. "I suffer from arthritis and can't do the chores as well as I used to. So she stays with us and shoulders most of those responsibilities."

Liesbet was a tall, slender woman with straight graying hair combed back into a knot. I judged her to be in her early fifties. In contrast, her older sister was slightly obese and of medium height, looking much older. They invited me to sit down. Both ladies joined me while I explained the reason for my visit. They wanted to see my products.

"What are the duties of a local distributor agent?" asked Liesbet.

They both listened intently as I explained what would be expected. Liesbet agreed to try it. I felt comfortable with her and looked forward to a pleasant working relationship.

"Where will you stay tonight?" asked Frau Goller as I got up to leave.

There were no public accommodations in Langenbach and the next town was six miles away. "I really don't know," was my reply. Getting to the next town would mean going over hill and dale on my trusty bike, and I was already tired.

"We have an extra bed upstairs," she said. "It sits in the hallway, and we go by there on our way to the bedrooms. If this doesn't bother you, we'd be pleased to have you stay here tonight."

"Thank you very much. I will accept your invitation."

It was 7 p.m. before I finished my route and returned to the Gollers' home. Frau Goller showed me the bed and location of the nearest washroom.

"Good night, Herr Hain. We eat breakfast at 7 a.m., please join us."

After I completed some paperwork and studying my Sabbath School lesson, I placed my Bible and quarterly on a nearby chair and soon fell asleep.

The next morning Herr Goller, a wiry man of medium height with thinning gray hair and hornedrimmed glasses joined the ladies. He appeared to be in his early sixties. Next to him sat Reinhold, their only son, then in his early thirties. Before we began breakfast, Herr Goller offered a brief prayer. While both men were polite and friendly, they left most of the conversation to the ladies.

Halfway through the meal, Liesbet turned to me with a curious look on her face. "What kind of booklet were you reading last night? I noticed a Bible too. What church do you attend?"

Aware that religious prejudice in that part of the country was alive and well, I had to formulate my reply carefully. The population of Bavaria was overwhelmingly Catholic. Towns and rural villages in Upper Franconia are either Catholic or Protestant with intermarriage strongly discouraged. The typical altars and pictures dedicated to the Virgin Mary were missing in the Langenbach homes. Herr Goller's prayer had been addressed to "Our Lord Jesus," and not "Holy Mary, Mother of God." Pretty sure I was eating with Protestants, most likely Lutherans, I continued.

"The church I attend refers to the booklet you saw as Sabbath School lessons, because we observe the seventh-day, Saturday, to worship God. I'm a Seventh-day Adventist."

Now everyone exchanged knowing glances. Liesbet rose from her chair, walked over to me, and gave me a big hug as she announced, "Lieber Bruder, wir sind auch Adventisten." Translated, this means, "Dear Brother, we too are Adventists."

What a pleasant surprise! I had not been aware of fellow believers in that part of the country, and she now informed me that some twenty church members regularly assembled for Sabbath worship in the Gollers living room.

Following this encounter, I had opportunity to worship with them on many occasions. We established a bond that endures to this day.

Chapter

4

A TEST OF FAITH

A few days before I was to leave for the Seminary in early September, 1951, a newly baptized church member, Elfriede Müller approached me to ask for financial assistance. We both lived in Wallenfels and had become acquainted during the series of Bible studies with Hans Zuber. While Elflriede was now also an enthusiastic Seventh-day Adventist, her husband wasn't pleased with her decision. He operated a trucking business while his wife handled the office chores. He feared she would spend valuable time away from home when he wanted her there. However, when problems developed with his truck, he had to decide whether to fix the old one or get a better one. His wife told him about me and the way I had been saving my money. So, they approached me for a loan.

"We just need enough to allow us to get a newer truck," they assured me. "We will pay you back when you need your money."

The amount they requested would take most of my

savings. Could I trust them to repay me when I needed my money? I had no question about Elfriede's sincere commitment. Her husband, however, was another matter. It seemed to me that he was always experiencing bad luck on the road. On the other hand, would he not need evidence that his wife's new faith was practical and Christians help one another?

Turning these matters over in my mind, I reviewed God's promise in Malachi 3 where He assures those who tithe faithfully, that the windows of heaven would be opened to them and not enough room to receive His blessings. I had been tithing faithfully since learning of this requirement during Hans Zuber's Bible studies. I also recalled reading in Matthew 5:42 the teachings of Jesus regarding lending. "Give to the one who asks you." Jesus had demanded in His Sermon on the Mount, "and do not turn away from the one who wants to borrow from you."

There was no doubt in my mind Herr Müller would judge our Christianity by the way I responded to their request. I could not disappoint them, so I agreed to loan them the money. Elfriede was quite pleased and promised to do all in her power to have it for me when I needed it.

"I'll see that your money earns interest," she added.

After writing the check to the Müllers and departing for Darmstadt, I knew what lay ahead. After making a limited down payment with help from mother, I requested employment on campus and inquired about other ways to earn money. I was told that ministerial students were given every Wednesday off to canvass surrounding towns, using the equivalents of *Signs of the Times* and *Life and Health* magazines. Also, I would have six weeks summer vacation to continue canvassing.

Chapter
5

MARIENHOEHE

Marienhoehe Seminary, the name meaning Mary's promontory, is located in an exclusive residential area south of Darmstadt, surrounded on three sides by coniferous forests. Orchards border the campus on the east side. Gently sloping hills ascend from the Rhine valley toward the *Odenwald* mountains, which stretch for 50 miles between Frankfurt and Heidelberg, reaching an elevation of 2,000 feet and giving the school a scenic backdrop. Numerous castles and medieval ruins make them a popular tourist attraction.

Streetcar tracks parallel a highway connecting downtown Darmstadt with Heidelberg and Frankfurt. Through a forest of evergreen trees, a well-worn path leads from the nearest streetcar stop to the school. The only road at that time skirted a United States Army Supply Depot and was not paved beyond it, discouraging all but essential traffic.

At the end of the path the forest opened to reveal a relatively small but well kept campus dominated by three main buildings with stucco finish. The largest structure facing east projected a semi-circular portico supported by five concrete pillars. The main floor contained a large assembly hall, a library, some classrooms, and the president's office. The two upper floors comprised the girl's dormitory. Dining room and kitchen facilities occupied the basement.

Connected to this building by a covered walkway, but facing north, was the tri-level school building with classrooms and faculty apartments. Further east at a higher elevation stood the tri-level men's dormitory.

Several narrow trails ascended to the forest that covered the summit of Mary's promontory. As I would eventually discover, many a student and some faculty members frequented these woods for both exercise and private devotions.

The high quality of education offered at Marienhoehe won friends among the educated citizens, as I discovered one Wednesday while canvassing in the area just east of the campus. I approached an ordinary-looking gentleman splitting wood in the backyard of an imposing home, only to find out he was the mayor of Darmstadt. Receiving me cordially, he purchased one of my magazines while praising the school I represented. Wishing me well, he said, "Moral values are important. Your people are doing a good work."

I was assigned a sparsely furnished room on the third floor of the men's dorm, sharing it with Helmut Maier, another theology student who later became a successful evangelist. The rising bell sounded at 6 a.m. and worship followed at 6:45 a.m., then breakfast at 7:15 a.m. Classes commenced at 8 a.m. and didn't end for some of us until mid-afternoon with only an hour for lunch. All students were expected to perform one hour of volunteer work per day, usually in the kitchen, the dining room, or on the grounds. Classes were held on Sundays so theology students could take Wednesdays off for canvassing.

Dating was discouraged for all but senior theology students. None of the girls studied theology, so our class composition was strictly male. Half of the female students lived in nearby towns and commuted to classes daily, so we hardly got to know them.

There were, however, some bright spots also. Seating in the dining room was rotated regularly. Three boys and three girls sat together for a month to practice their social skills. Weather permitting, faculty and students participated in long Sabbath afternoon hikes, sometimes into the distant Odenwald mountains with its ancient castles. Many friendships were thus developed and some romances ignited. It was strenuous activity and the faculty's way of *"wearing out the saints"* so that Saturday night study periods were not interrupted by forbidden behavior.

Toward the school year's end there was the annual banquet. Those who hoped, during this event, to sit with their *"special friends"* were usually disappointed. The young men, upon entering the banquet hall, were asked to draw a folded piece of paper from a basket. Inside was a girl's name, their date for the evening. Thus no student was left out. Attempts to switch partners were not tolerated.

Our food was adequate but commensurate with the times. For breakfast we were served hot cereal and white buns that we ate with jam and margarine. The noon meals featured mostly soups made from potatoes, legumes, and other vegetables. Sometimes potatoes were boiled and served with *"quark,"* a kind of cottage cheese. On rare occasions we were fed fish. Evening meals resembled lunch except that different varieties of cheese were provided for the bread. The most common beverage was a Postum-like coffee substitute.

Tiring of the dining room food, I struck up a friendship with Karin, an attractive Home Economics major. She encouraged me to join a one-semester cooking class during my second year at Marienhoehe. We met once a week for an entire afternoon, preparing a full-course dinner, then enjoying the results. Even if our offerings were sometimes burnt or otherwise less than perfect, they were far superior to our routine fare in the dining room. Without Karin's help, I would have never received a passing grade.

At the conclusion of the course the entire class, four boys, four girls and a teacher, took a trip to the city of Wiesbaden, where we spent the better part of the day at its famous Botanical Gardens. Later we had dinner in an upscale restaurant. Our trusted teacher outdid herself in her capacity as chaperone. On the way home Karin and I had a long discussion. Becoming a minister's wife was not one of her ambitions, she told me. Of course, I was deeply disappointed.

A highlight of my time at the seminary was acting as translator for visiting Americans. Since Frankfurt, seat of the American High Command, was only 25 miles away and an Army Supply Depot practically next door, it was not uncommon to have visitors on campus who spoke very little German. During the church services I often sat next to American servicemen at the back of the assembly room and translated the sermons. Afterwards, many of them would join us for dinner and later on hikes. Since not many of the students could converse in English, I functioned as interpreter for them as well. This provided welcome opportunities for co-educational interchange.

At the end of my first year, I befriended Goswin

Rosenblüh, an athletic theology major. We decided to canvass together in Swabia, part of southern Germany, where his parents lived. He made arrangements for us to stay with an elderly Adventist couple in the city of Pforzheim, known for its manufacture of watches and cuckoo clocks. We hoped that a low unemployment rate in that area would assure us sales success. However, other salesmen had the same idea, making people gun-shy of anyone trying to sell something.

There were usually three apartments on each of the five floors of residential buildings. People watched from peepholes whenever anyone rang a bell on their floor and decided right then whether or not to open their door. We had to find a way around this.

"Let's visit only the apartments on the left side as we go up, then the ones on the right on our way down. Finally, we go up again and do the center ones," Goswin suggested.

"What good will that do?"

"It will confuse them," he insisted.

"It's worth a try." I responded reluctantly, because this would slow us down. There were no elevators.

This approach gained us entrance into some of the apartments. We arranged several issues of magazines in packages selling for DM 2.-, 3.-, and more. We set our goal at 50 DM per day. If we sold that amount we could earn most of our tuition in the six weeks we had available.

Our work was rewarding, but tiring. We found that drinking milk and eating plain yogurt helped replenish our energy. Our hosts provided breakfast and supper. We patronized local cafes for our noon meals.

Weekends were spent at Goswin's home in a little village east of Pforzheim. We attended church with them in the mornings and hiked into the countryside on Sabbath afternoons. Goswin's father served on the police force and took along his dog, Prinz, a German Shepherd. Goswin's one sister worked away from home during the week but sometimes joined us for our walks. She too was trying to earn her tuition and planned to attend classes at Marienhoehe.

Chapter
6

FIRE IN THE DORM

Back on campus, ready to begin my second year, I was surprised by the news that all theology students were being moved into a former Army barrack south of the high school building. Instead of two persons to each room, we now shared space with six others. Walls were thin and heating less than adequate on cold days. There were four rooms of equal size and another, smaller one near the entrance for our Dean. As a second-year student I was assigned the first room to the right upon entering the building. Two windows faced toward the north. I chose a site directly underneath a window.

Walter, our Dean, was a recent convert from Lutheranism and graduate of one of their seminaries. He had a hard time adjusting to our food, choosing instead to prepare his own on a hot plate in his room, something none of the rest of us were allowed to do. He was small of stature, rosy cheeked, and wore a perpetual smile whenever he spoke in his heavy Swabian accent.

About half way through the school year, on a Wednesday morning, while most of the students were canvassing in surrounding towns, Walter was using his hot plate to fix breakfast. When a stiff breeze slammed his apartment door shut, he was attempting to reopen it when a window curtain made contact with the hot plate and caught fire. Flames spread quickly and soon engulfed the entire room. Despite his valiant efforts and that of others who were quickly summoned, the building burned to the ground.

Fortunately for me, because my bed was near a window, most of my possessions were easily grabbed and thrown out before the flames reached that spot. Others were less fortunate. Yet, some valuables were recovered from the rubble over the next day or two. One student found his Bible, unharmed with tithe money still inside. Others found important documents singed, but still usable.

At a long prayer and praise service, some shed tears and others recommitted their lives to Christ. Faculty and students united in thanking God that no lives were lost.

Where was I that day? Using the streetcar, I had left right after breakfast to canvass one of the nearby towns. A few days before I had taken my portable typewriter downtown for cleaning and planned to pick it up that night. Some senior theology students had urged me to see a movie they had viewed a few days before, claiming it was a must-see kind of event. Portrayed by James Mason, a British actor, the movie told the story of Field Marshall Rommel as DESERT FOX. I was always interested in military stories, and this one in particular as one of my cousins served under Rommel in North Africa and was later captured by British forces. Rommel was highly respected by both sides and later died at the hands of the SS—for opposing Hitler.

Being fully aware that I was breaking a cardinal rule of the school by visiting a public movie theater, I yielded to the temptation. Entering the theater, typewriter in hand, I sat in the back seat and watched the reenactment of Rommel's North African battles. It was dark when I made my way from the streetcar stop and walked through the woods back to school.

Arriving on campus shortly before 9 p.m., I sensed that something was wrong. A small group of students huddled together on the lawn in front of the main building, conversing in subdued tones. With a guilty conscience, I made myself as inconspicuous as I could while walking toward the barracks. Rounding the corner of the high school building, I stopped short. No barrack! Just a lone chimney reaching toward the starlit sky. In front of me, still smoldering, lay the ruins of what had been, until a few hours ago, home to 30 theology students.

I was deeply shocked and humiliated. Assigned to share a room with two very committed senior theology students in the main dormitory for the rest of the school year, I resolved to observe all rules.

Chapter
7

BIBLE STUDIES

The fire left a lasting impression in my mind. I became convinced that I should find people with whom to study the Bible. God had obviously allowed this disaster to reinforce my dependence on Him just as He had delivered me during the air raid in central Germany. I shared my feelings with Eddy, who supervised student colporteurs. He agreed. "You have something worthwhile to share," he said.

"I'd like to visit some of the American families who live nearby," I proposed. "They usually employ German housekeepers. I could try selling them our magazines and maybe even *Lebensbilder*, the four-volume set of character building stories."

"Don't forget *Life and Health*, which is available in English," he reminded me with a grin.

Eddy had warmed to the idea and now invited me to pray with him, seeking guidance from God. I left his office determined to proceed with my plan.

For the next several weeks I experimented with numerous approaches, targeting primarily Germans who worked for Americans. Some bought the magazines. Most did not. Then I approached American housewives with the idea of buying *Lebensbilder* as gifts for their hired German help for Christmas. This worked a little better but demanded more time for my book demonstrations. Finally, I just prayed that God would help me find people who were searching for Biblical truths. I had taken numerous Bible subjects at school and wanted to share what I had learned. My prayer was answered one Wednesday in early December.

It was nearly noon when I approached the last house on a dead-end street. A fence surrounded the property. When I rang the bell, two dogs emerged, barking furiously while they jumped up and down on the other side of the gate. *Another home that needs dogs to keep salesmen away*, I thought.

A lady dressed in slacks and wearing a pleasant smile opened the door. She appeared to be in her thirties. Commanding the dogs to retreat, she invited: "Come in! You mustn't be offended at the dogs. It's their way of saying, 'hello.' I'm Mrs. Cramer. What brings you here?"

Before I could explain, another woman's voice, speaking German, interrupted from inside: "Wer is da?" ("Who is it?")

I mused to myself, *this will be interesting!*

"Oh, somebody wants to talk to us, Mother," replied Mrs. Cramer in German.

"You don't mind if I join the conversation in the language so familiar to both of you?" I inquired.

"Not at all," said Mrs. Cramer as she introduced Mrs. Specker. "We are both Swiss citizens, but I am married to an American official."

At once I showed them *Lebensbilder*, emphasizing the importance of raising children with high moral values. "These make excellent Christmas gifts for grandchildren," I added, thinking Mrs. Specker might be interested.

To my surprise, Mrs. Specker agreed to purchase a set for another daughter in Switzerland. When I offered personal delivery, Mrs. Cramer suggested that I meet her husband, who, she assured me, was interested in religious subjects. We agreed on December 18, a few days before I would leave for Christmas vacation.

When I called at the Cramer residence next time to deliver my books, a tall gentleman greeted me. He stood with military bearing but was dressed in civilian clothes.

"This is my husband," interjected Mrs. Cramer.

After shaking hands, he looked me over carefully, a curious smile on his face. "So you are the fellow with the books on religion, are you?" he said still grinning. "I hope you brought some spare time along. Come into the living room with me." There he handed me a beautifully illustrated jubilee edition of the King James Bible and sat down beside me.

For the next hour we talked about the inspiration of the Bible and about Jesus. I learned that Mr. Cramer had good knowledge of the Scriptures. He had been attending various churches but was not satisfied with their doctrines.

"With most of them, it's just a matter of asking for money," he insisted. "What church do you belong to?"

"I'm Seventh-day Adventist."

"Never heard of them," he said. "What do they teach?"

By the time I finished summarizing our major doctrines, it was 9:55 p.m.

"Sorry, Mr. Cramer, but I have exactly five minutes to reach the dormitory before curfew. If I don't leave now, I may not make it." We both stood up.

"Let me drive you. It will give us more time to talk."

In the car he showed a sincere desire to know more. We agreed to meet again following Christmas vacation.

A thick layer of new snow covered the countryside in January. I found Mr. and Mrs. Cramer, along with Mrs. Specker, ready for Bible study. Our topic was "The Plan of Salvation."

Noticing that Mrs. Specker was not able to follow in English, I translated each point into German. This took extra time but I wanted Mrs. Specker to be included in our discussion. They invited me back the following Wednesday evening.

Our second study dealt with Bible prophecy. Mr. Cramer became quite enthusiastic about Daniel 2. "I've never in my life heard the Bible explained in this manner," he said.

During our next visit, I left several pamphlets and a two-volume edition of *Daniel and the Revelation*, by Uriah Smith. I gave some German pamphlets to Mrs. Specker. Three weeks later Mr. Cramer returned the books.

"I've read them through," he announced, obviously pleased.

After covering several other topics at weekly intervals, I sensed it was time to examine health principles. I had noticed the Cramers were fond of tobacco, tea, coffee, and pork. Asking the Lord for extra help in presenting this important subject, I looked for an opportunity to introduce it as convincingly and attractively as possible. The opportunity came sooner than I expected.

Mrs. Cramer turned to me suddenly, "Say, how did you ever come to believe all the things you're telling us? You say you come from a Lutheran background. I've been a Lutheran all my life and I know our church members don't change their religion overnight."

While recounting my own conversion, emphasizing the changes in my eating and drinking habits, I especially focused on my break with tobacco.

Astonished, Mrs. Cramer shot a quizzical look at her husband, "I suppose I should stop smoking cigarettes, then? And you should quit your cigars too, honey." She continued, "The young man is right about their harmful effect."

Mrs. Specker interjected, "As far as pork is concerned, my doctor doesn't permit me to eat any of it, which goes to show that it is detrimental to good health."

I proceeded to prove from the Bible that our bodies are temples of the Holy Spirit and that God requires them to be kept clean. All three seemed impressed. Mrs. Cramer put out a freshly lit cigarette, "Well if that's what the Bible says, I am quitting right now!" She looked at her husband, "Well, honey, how about it?"

"If you can quit cigarettes, then I can quit cigars," he said resolutely.

"We'll quit together," she said with determination written all over her face.

And quit they did. The next time I came to their home, the ashtrays were gone. As Mr. Cramer drove me home, I missed the strong aroma of his cigars in the car. God had performed another miracle!

The rest of the story is quickly told. The whole family accepted the truths brought to them from week to week. Soon they would be ready for baptism. Mr.

Cramer had a responsible position at the Army Supply Depot. He had to apply for Sabbath privileges, but God helped him get that settled.

On my last visit with the Cramers at the end of the school year, Elder Schwital, my favorite Bible teacher, accompanied me to their home. He agreed to carry on with the studies. The Cramers responded well to his visits and were eventually baptized.

I look back fondly on those Marienhoehe years where I met some of my best teachers, like Ms. Untritz, the unassuming and multi-talented teacher from Riga in Latvia who not only spoke twelve languages but also taught Greek and Hebrew.

Elder Dangschadt's enthusiasm while preaching was truly contagious. I still recall the essential points of the first sermon I ever heard him give shortly after arriving on campus. It was the Elijah message on Mount Carmel to the worshipers of Baal. He concluded with a stirring appeal, "Whose side are you on?"

The influence of many others, both teachers and students, still lingers. Visitors like William Bergherm, a United States Army Chaplain, could hold a youthful audience spellbound while recounting the story of Jesus. And Franz Hasel, at that time Publishing Secretary of the Central European Division, addressed the students frequently, inspiring them to share the message via the printed page. His daughter, Susi, has since written a book, *A Thousand Shall Fall*, detailing her father's remarkable deliverance during World War II when he served in the German Army, without ever using a weapon. I thank God for all of these people.

Chapter
8

GOOD-BYE GERMANY!

At the conclusion of my second school year at Marenhoehe, I returned to Wallenfels. I had reasons to be grateful. God had blessed my canvassing work and allowed me to leave school with all bills paid. Now I had to consider the next step. Where should I continue my education?

While attending the cooking classes, I had befriended Axel Johnson, a Swedish student who was planning to study at Canadian Union College in Alberta, Canada.

"It's a good school and not expensive," Axel assured me. "Why don't you consider going there? I can give you the address of the president."

CANADA! How well I remembered receiving a package with an almost new suit and other good quality clothes from the Dorcas ladies in Saskatoon, Saskatchewan, shortly after my baptism. I was attending church wearing a dyed GI uniform, causing some members to feel sorry for me. The head elder contacted relatives in

Saskatoon, requesting more appropriate garments for this new convert. If Canadians were as generous and kind as those who sent the package, perhaps I could take the chance and go there, I reasoned.

June was almost over when I finally wrote to Mr. H.T. Johnson, President of the Canadian Union College, explaining my intentions but adding, "I will have to find a job on campus and would like to canvass as soon as I can after arrival. My financial resources are extremely limited." I shared how God had blessed my canvassing in Germany.

"If you take care of paying your bills, we'll take care of you. Come on over." Mr. Johnson wrote back. "I'll see that you meet Elder Russ Spangler, our Conference Publishing Secretary."

My departure for a land so far away would be difficult for Mutti, as she still depended on my help sometimes. Uncle Willi had remarried and now lived in Westfalia where Aunt Grete and her five children had found a new home. Mutti felt isolated from her family.

"Maybe you can follow me later on," I suggested.

"You speak English and I'm too old to learn a new language," she said with tears welling up in her eyes.

"You could join Willi and Grete! You know how to work and good workers are always in demand," I said, trying to encourage her.

While negotiating with the various airlines, I quickly learned that most of them preferred dollars to marks. I would certainly need the money I had loaned to the Müllers for their truck.

Mutti informed me that the Müllers had been having a lot of misfortunes lately, and that she was worried about my money not being available. "Leave it to the Lord," I assured her. "God knows I need it now.

After all, we helped them when they needed it."

The day came when I had to visit the Müllers. Fortunately, Herr Müller was on the road. I knew he resented me ever since his wife joined our church. He was a staunch Catholic. Elfriede greeted me warmly. "I know why you're here," she said. "Just give me a minute." With that she disappeared into one of the bedrooms, emerging moments later with an envelope in hand. It was a check.

"It's the full amount plus interest," she announced with a big smile. "We are having a tough time in our business again, but God will take care of that in His own way. You need to get on with your education. Our best wishes and sincere prayers go with you."

* * *

There was only one travel agency in Wallenfels. We had no telephone, so all negotiations had to be done in person. At first the agent suggested booking an ocean liner that would sail on August 6. Before that date, I would need an acceptance letter from the college and a student visa from the Canadian Consulate in Frankfurt. All this took several weeks and meant a trip to Frankfurt. I'll never forget the Consul's expression when he asked me, "Where in, _____, is College Heights?" He had never heard of it, but issued the required document.

School would begin during the first week of October. I needed at least six weeks to earn money for registration and tuition expenses. This called for my arrival at Canadian Union College (CUC) before August 15. Going by boat was out.

After the agent had tried several airlines, he announced, "*Air France* will accept German currency.

Somebody canceled a booking on August 13, probably based on superstitions. If you can make that date, we'll hold it for you."

He didn't have to ask me twice; I accepted it immediately. It was an answer to my prayer. It would take most of my money. I also needed to pay for rail transportation from Montreal to Lacombe in Canada.

The morning of August 13 arrived all too quickly. The train was to leave at 8:15 a.m. Elfriede and her two daughters, Christa (16) and Brigitte (15), insisted on helping by pushing their bicycles loaded with our luggage all the way to the Wallanfels railroad station. Mutti arranged to accompany me to the airport in Frankfurt. Following my departure, she would stay with some church members in the city for a few more days.

It was not easy to part with the Müllers, for we were all members of God's family and shared the same hope and faith. Elfriede had a tough row to hoe with her unbelieving husband. The girls, after hearing me talk about Canada, expressed their desire to cross the ocean too someday. Years later, they did.

We had a brief prayer together before entering the station, asking God to direct our paths and allow us to meet again, if not on this earth, then in heaven. After boarding our train and finding a window seat, Mutti and I waved as long as we could see those precious friends.

We arrived at the Rhine-Main airport with plenty of time to check my luggage and do more visiting. Mutti was having difficulty controlling her emotions. She had lost two husbands, a home with a large garden, and now was about to part with her only child.

"We can be grateful that Aunt Grete and Uncle Willi are alive and comfortably situated in Westfalia,"

I said trying to be cheerful. "They want you to live near them."

"I know. But they are not church members and don't care for this *new* religion we practice."

"True," I agreed. "Yet being with family is a lot better than living all alone and far from them. Besides, think of this as an opportunity to share your newfound faith. They need God too! Why don't you take a trip up there and look around. If they find accommodations and a job for you, move!"

Mutti had legitimate reasons for her concerns. At this time, she had a steady job at the Wallenfels Elementary School, preparing one hot meal per day for the students. It provided food for her as well. And she had a supportive church family.

"Whatever happens, always remember how the Lord got us through the train wreck and how He helped us recover our bicycles," I said consolingly.

"It's so hard to see you go this far away," her voice trembled. "Will I ever see you again?"

"Let's leave that in God's hands. If at all possible, I will try to arrange for you to follow me. It may take awhile, but I'll do my best."

It was time to board the plane. We hugged once more. Her voice steady now and hope reflected in her eyes, she bade me good-bye. "Go with God, my son."

Once inside the plane, I secured a window seat from which I could watch the people lining up near the administration building, waving farewell. Among them was Mutti.

Chapter
9

UNEXPECTED DELAY

My attention now shifted to the airplane. This was my first experience flying. I had built and flown model airplanes, but never left the ground before. This was the real thing! I was excited.

The DC-4, its four engines roaring, began to move toward the runway. Arriving there, the captain revved up the engines, causing the plane to vibrate and groan under the stress. Receiving clearance from the control tower, he released the brakes and we were on our way. Faster and faster the plane surged forward until, at last, we were airborne. The buildings disappeared from view behind us. The landscape below grew smaller as we gained altitude. Soon the captain turned off the NO SMOKING sign and flew toward Paris. What an amazing way to travel, leaving behind congested highways and angry drivers! We landed at Orley airport in a little more than an hour.

After leaving the plane we were greeted by disturbing news. "Paris is on strike," came a voice over the loudspeakers. We were to report to our airline ticket counters for further information.

"There will be no flights to Montreal tonight," they told me. "We don't know when or if there will be any tomorrow." My heart sank. "Check with us tomorrow." The airline gave us coupons which entitled us to three meals and one night's stay in a downtown hotel and bus transportation.

Later that evening, the waiters at the hotel exchanged surprised glances when I refused meat and alcohol. There was plenty of fruit, which I consumed instead. My room had no air conditioning, but it did have a big window. I opened it to let in some fresh air. My eardrums pulsated from the loud jazz music from downstairs. I had a choice: Either get the fresh air and tolerate the music, or close the window and deal with a stuffy interior. I chose the fresh air. Fully exhausted from the excitement of the day, I soon fell asleep, grateful to God. I prayed He would see me through to Canada in time to earn the needed funds for school.

The next day, the news was no better. We were delayed yet another night and were given more coupons and another night's lodging in the same hotel. The airlines told us they would only pay for three days and nights.

It was now Friday and I wondered where to spend Sabbath. While taking a walk I found a little store that carried health foods. The proprietor spoke no English, but one of the young customers, a student, came to my aid repeating my request for the address of the nearest Seventh-day Adventist church. Between the two they came up with an address, which the student wrote on a piece of paper. I thanked him for his assistance.

The next morning, after a breakfast of fruit and hot cereal, I hailed a taxi and went to church. It was not a large building, but the congregation was friendly and made me feel at home. A deacon translated the sermon from French into English for me and later escorted me to a potluck meal. When I expressed concern about accommodation after Saturday night, he offered his phone number. "Call me if you get stuck. We can set up a bunk bed downstairs in one of the children's divisions."

Encouraged by his hospitality, I left the church and returned to the hotel. From my room I called the *Air France* agency and was told that there would be a plane leaving for Montreal at 10:05 that night but that all the seats were sold out. The agent explained that not all their passengers had been notified, and there was a slight chance I might get on.

By 9:30 p.m. I was at the airport, joining a noisy group of excited travelers who congregated in front of the gate marked, "MONTREAL." While waiting, I made the acquaintance of two Americans, one named Don, a businessman from New York, and the other Curtis, from Los Angeles, also on business. I shared my concerns to get to Alberta as soon as possible so I could earn money for college. They listened sympathetically and promised to help.

"When the gate opens," said Don, "we'll walk forward together with you in the middle. Once on the plane, we'll go to the tail section. The stewardesses will start at the front checking tickets, by the time they get to us, we'll be airborne."

"I hope this plan works," I replied sheepishly, feeling a little guilty.

The gate finally opened at 10:30 p.m. and the crowd surged forward en masse. Everyone clutching a ticket and holding them up for the agent to see. He could not possibly look at every ticket. Helplessly, he motioned for us to go on. With Don and Curtis on either side of me, I squeezed through the gate and rushed into the plane, where we found seats in the tail section as planned. There were three rows of seats on either side of the aisle. I chose one next to the window because I wanted to see America, this New World, when it came into view. Don and Curtis sat next to me.

True to Don's word, a stewardess now began in front checking tickets. She had to stop when we taxied to the runway and took off. She didn't resume her investigation until the plane reached cruising altitude. We were aboard a *Conny*, a four-engine Constellation equipped with three vertical stabilizers. It was a noisy plane, especially while climbing. When the stewardess came to our row, we all handed her our tickets. She examined mine a bit more closely, gave me an odd look, tore part of it off, and then handed the stub back without comment. She apparently noticed that my name was not on her list of registered passengers. I was occupying a seat of a passenger who either was too late getting on board or one who just didn't claim it. Either way, the seat was mine now. When she had gone, Don turned to me, "It worked, didn't it!"

Smiling, I agreed as we settled down for the long journey ahead. Both stressed out and excited, I just couldn't sleep. The moment I had been dreaming about since childhood was about to become reality. I would actually enter the continent of North America! My seatmates were both sleeping when we descended into Reykjavik, the capital of Iceland for refueling. It was shortly after 2 a.m., August 16, 1953.

Most of the passengers remained on the plane. Forty-five minutes later we were back in the air, the North Atlantic Ocean below. When the sun came up, we were flying over land. "Labrador," Curtis informed me. I couldn't see any evidence of human habitations.

I had yet to grasp the immense size of North America. A mere 15 million people lived in Canada at that time compared to the 75 million squeezed into East and West Germany, which would fit into Canada more than ten times over!

At 11 a.m., the captain announced, "Ladies and gentlemen, we are descending on Montreal. Please fasten your seat belts."

Chapter
10

CANADA — HERE I COME!

We touched down in Montreal shortly after 12 noon. Since we were seated in the rear of the plane, it took awhile to disembark. I asked Curtis to take my picture with the plane in the background. He gladly complied before getting back on. He and Don would continue toward New York City. I thanked both earnestly for what they had done for me. They wished me good luck in my studies.

I immediately noticed that I was in the French-speaking part of Canada. The signs were in both English and French. While going through customs, I heard most everyone using French, but the officials also spoke English and I was soon on my way to hail a taxi.

Elder Russ Spangler, Publishing Secretary of the Alberta Conference, had sent me the address of the Montreal Adventist Church and the name of the caretaker. I call him Frank, since I have since forgotten his name. Frank was a kindhearted man in his 70s. The church was located on the outskirts of the city in a multi-level brick structure. A widower, he occupied the second level, with the sanctuary on the main floor. I was to spend my first night and part of the next day with him. He provided food and a comfortable bed, and didn't seem to mind when I asked to be allowed to sleep. Jet lag had finally caught up with me.

The next morning, after breakfast, Frank took me downtown to help me buy a pair of shoes, which I desperately needed. I also bought some fruit for the trip to Alberta. By mid-afternoon he delivered me to the railway station and made sure I got on the train for Calgary.

"When you get to Calgary, you need to change trains. The conductor will help you. Good-bye." With that Frank was gone.

The scenery from Montreal to Calgary was very different from Europe. There, everything is crowded. Here the countryside seemed sparsely settled. While traveling through Ontario, the predominance of forest and lakes reminded me of James Fenimore Cooper's *Leatherstocking Tales*, which I had read during my third year of high school English. I tried to imagine what it must have been like when trappers and Indians stalked deer, elk, and each other in these endless woods and paddled their canoes on the rivers we now crossed at great speed on the train.

While crossing the Prairie Provinces, with their wide-open spaces and often no trees, I engaged some of my fellow passengers in conversations regarding Indians. "They live on reservations," said a passenger sitting across from me. "It's not a healthful situation. The Government gives them a monthly check, money they all too often squander on alcohol instead of using it to improve their homes and dietary habits."

"Do they still wear their feather headgear and buckskin clothes?" I asked curiously.

"Only during special ceremonies and for parades," a seatmate told me. "Since you are going to Alberta, be sure to visit the Calgary Stampede, which takes place every June," he said. "There you can see Indians in their native dress and you can crawl into their tee-pees."

"And what about cowboys?" I asked.

"You'll see plenty of them there and watch their chuck wagon races."

"Do they wear six-shooters?"

That question met with a patronizing glance. "It's not like what you see in the movies. Today, they use a revolver to shoot a snake or wild animal, but not people."

By the time we arrived in Calgary, where I had to change trains, my ideas of the Old West had changed quite a bit. There were no cowboys riding around with six-shooters strapped to their belts engaging Indians in battle for new lands. I concluded that Karl May, an au-thor known throughout Germany for his Indian tales, which I devoured as a kid, missed Canada.

While the Old West had changed considerably, my desire to explore and see for myself hadn't. I had to remind myself that, first and foremost, I was here to study.

Chapter
11

CANADIAN UNION COLLEGE (CUC)

The train pulled into Lacombe before noon on Thursday, August 20. It had taken me four days and three nights from Montreal. There to meet me with a gray Ford pick-up truck was a tall, chubby gentleman whom I judged to be in his late twenties. He scrutinized all passengers getting off the train and then zeroed in on me.

"Are you Hain?" he asked.

"Yes," I replied as I extended my hand to shake his.

"I'm Willis Clark. Welcome to Canadian Union College," he said, shaking my hand. "Let's get your luggage and go on up to the school. You are still in time for dinner."

Dinner sounded good to me. On our way we passed through part of Lacombe, then a town of about 2,500 population. Willis drove northward on a paved road for another three miles, then turned west onto College Avenue, as he called it. That road was not paved, and riddled with potholes. The pickup rattled and shook mercilessly. Clouds of dust we kicked up drifted toward nearby homes.

"The road needs grading," said Willis grinning in response to the horror reflected on my face. "You'll get used to it after awhile." He pointed out the main auditorium where church services were conducted as he drove me to the dormitory. Farther on we passed two huge barns with bright red roofs.

"That's our farm," he announced proudly. "The college owns several hundred head of cattle, and some of our students earn their tuition by milking cows."

I had never seen barns that size nor heard of a school that owned hundreds of cattle. I was genuinely impressed. A short distance south stood the administration building that, according to Willis, housed offices, classrooms, and a spacious chapel. It occupied the central part of the campus and was flanked on the east by the girls dorm and on the west by the boy's dorm.

Willis stopped the truck at the base of a steep stairway that led to the main entrance of the men's dormitory, called West Hall. He helped carry my luggage to the second floor where a room had been reserved for me. It was furnished with a bunk bed, table, chairs, closet, and a sink. A window provided an enticing view of a nearby lake.

"Bathrooms are down the hall," said Willis. "Make sure you get to the cafeteria before 1 p.m. You'll also need to set up an account for charging meals." Before he left, he showed me how to get to the cafeteria and also to the president's office.

The cafeteria building formed part of the southeastern rim of the campus and looked down on a sparsely settled valley bordered by a lake on either side. The town of Lacombe formed a picturesque backdrop.

When I arrived in the cafeteria, ten minutes before closing time, most of the students who worked on campus had left. Only a few lingered at one table and looked up as I entered and stared curiously. Behind the tray line counter, a middle-aged lady with graying hair and friendly smile waited to serve me.

"I just arrived here from Germany and don't have a meal ticket yet." I told her, "But I can pay cash."

"That won't be necessary," she replied. "We'll charge your meals to your account that you set up in the business office."

That was easy, I mused to myself while selecting a baked potato, several vegetables, and a meat substitute made from wheat gluten, which was a new experience for me. I chose bread pudding for dessert, and milk for a drink. The water had a slightly sulfuric taste. While the quality and variety of food here was superior to that of Mariehoehe, I missed the heavy, dark brown bread of Germany.

By the time I sat down to eat, the other students had left. As the only guest, I now had the freedom to sit wherever I wished. I selected a table from which I could enjoy the view.

In the distance, several grain elevators near the railroad station stood like sentinels guarding the entrance to Lacombe. A vast expanse of golden grain fields and green pastures with widely scattered farms stretched gently upward toward the eastern horizon. It was a tranquil scene, hardly disturbed by the shrill whistle of a freight train puffing its way north toward Edmonton, the provincial capital. To my extreme right, I could make out the southern tip of the lake that enhanced the view from my dormitory room. Lake Barnett, Willis had called it. The lady who had served me the food interrupted my reverie.

"I'm Helen Sahly, wife of the Director of Food Service," she said smiling warmly. "Mind if I join you for a few minutes?"

"Not at all, I was just admiring the scenery."

"You say you just arrived from Germany?"

"Well, I left there a week ago and was delayed in Paris so it took me awhile to get here."

"I understand." She said. "We have a daughter, Orene, who is dating a young man with relatives in Germany. His name is David Igler."

Could he be a relative of the two Igler families with whom I had worshiped after joining the Adventist church? They had mentioned relatives in Canada who had a son, but they referred to him as Roland.

"Where does David live?" I asked.

"In Saskatoon, Saskatchewan."

"I've heard of a Roland Igler."

"That's the one! He prefers David, but his birth name is Roland."

"Is he here now?" I asked with excitement.

"No, but we expect him when school starts."

"Great!" I was hardly able to contain my enthusiasm. "I certainly want to meet him and I'll tell you why. You see, my mother and I are refugees from East Germany and lost practically everything to the Russians. After becoming Adventists, we started attending church in a little Bavarian town called Klein-Vichtach, about six miles from where we lived. We met with a group of 10 to 12 believers in a private home owned by Reinhold Igler. His brother, Heinrich, is the church elder. Because I had worked for the American Army before my conversion, I still wore one of their uniforms, dyed navy blue, to church. Apparently, this caused some concerns, because several months later I received a package from Saskatoon, Canada, with almost new clothes, including a suit that fit me perfectly. It was a gift from the Saskatoon Dorcas Society. Their leader is wife to another Igler brother. Your daughter's friend is related to the Iglers I know in Germany!"

"What a coincidence," she said excited. "We must get better acquainted. You must meet my husband, Joe. He still speaks a bit of German."

"I look forward to that." Feeling grateful for such a turn of events. I quickly finished eating and went to the administration building to find the business office. Near the flowerbeds, south of the building, I noticed a little girl playing, perhaps seven or eight years old. She gave me a curious look as I passed her and then asked, "What's you name?"

Always charmed by the sound of children's voices speaking in a foreign language I replied, "My name is Dieter Hain."

"My mommy told me about you. Daddy is the president and mommy is his secretary."

"I'm on my way to see your daddy," I told her, duly impressed by her friendliness. "What's your name?"

"I'm Carole Johnson."

"It's nice meeting you, Carole," I said while moving toward the main entrance. Sprinting up the stairwell, I almost bumped into a lady on her way down. She wore a long dress, short hair and glasses. I greeted her smiling and slightly out of breath. Guessing, I said, "Would you be Mrs. Johnson?"

"Yes I am," she replied, keeping her professional reserve. "How did you know?"

"Your charming little daughter alerted me. She says you are the president's secretary." This brought a smile to her face.

"And you are?"

"I'm Dieter Hain."

"Welcome to Canadian Union College. We've been expecting you."

I shook her hand firmly. "Thank you, ma'am! Perhaps you could direct me to your husband's office?"

"Turn left at the top of the stairs. His is the first office on your left."

With that she turned and continued down the steps. Moments later I knocked on Mr. Johnson's office door. He invited me in, rose to his feet, and extended his hand.

After I introduced myself, he said, "Welcome to Canada! I've been expecting you. Have a seat," he motioned toward a couch across from his desk. He was a man of medium height with a high forehead and a receding hairline. He must have been in his late 40's at that time. He wore a gray business suit and rimless glasses. His speech was rapid but clear as he gave me his full attention. "So you want to start canvassing right away?" He asked.

"Yes sir! Not later than Monday, but I will need help from the Publishing Secretary. How can I contact him?"

"Let's take care of that right now," he said as he reached for the telephone. Before he hung up, the matter was settled. Elder Russ Spangler would meet me after breakfast on Monday in front of West Hall. "You'll have about six weeks to earn your scholarship."

"What do you mean, scholarship?" I asked.

"Arrangements between the college and the Alberta Conference, guaranteeing your educational expenses for the next school year, provided you work a certain number of hours and sell a certain amount of literature," he explained. "Based on your experience in Germany, I'm sure you can do it."

"Thank you for your vote of confidence, and with God's help, I will do my best."

He continued, "By the way, how would you like to speak at our vesper service tomorrow night? We don't have many people coming right now, but I'm sure they would like to hear your story."

"I have never conducted a service in English before," I objected.

"There's nothing wrong with your English." He smiled. "Be at the assembly room of West Hall tomorrow night at 7:30 p.m., I'll introduce you." It was settled.

Before I left, Mr. Johnson directed me to the business office where a charge account was set up for me to cover my expenses until registration day. I felt relieved for my cash reserve had dwindled to less than $20.

I spent considerable time preparing my vesper sermon. True to his promise, Mr. Johnson introduced me to a group of about 30 people the next evening. It was a mixture of faculty, students, and local residents who chose to attend during summer months. Using Hebrews 11, I attempted to illustrate the meaning of faith by recalling God's leading in my life, especially during the past few weeks. The audience was responsive and Mr. Johnson seemed pleased.

The next day, Sabbath, I worshipped with the College Heights congregation in the auditorium. I was slowly getting used to praying and singing in English. The previous Sabbath I had been surrounded by French-speaking believers.

During my noon meal, I was joined by Joe Sahly, a jovial rotund gentleman, small of stature with a round face, wearing a chef's hat and white apron.

"Du bist ein Deutscher?" he asked in German while shaking my hand. "Ich versteh ein wenig." (You are German? I understand a little.) His pronunciation indicated Swabian ancestry. He quizzed me about my past and future plans and wanted to know more about Dave Igler's family in Germany. "That young man is going places," he predicted, apparently pleased that his daughter was *going steady* with him.

Chapter

12

MORE CANVASSING

On Monday morning Elder Spangler was waiting in his car outside the dorm when I returned from breakfast. He was a man of medium height and build. He wore a brown suit and dark rimmed glasses and his hair combed straight back. His intense manner was due to the heavy responsibilities resting on his shoulders. That summer he supervised more than 10 student *colporteurs* in addition to his *regulars*.

"I blocked off this entire day for you," he assured me. "Every sale we make will be credited to you!" After insisting that I take my clothes and toilet articles along, we departed for the hamlet of Mirror, southeast of Lacombe. There he chose to visit the families living in house trailers, convinced that they would more likely order children's books. By noon he had sold three sets of *Uncle Arthur's Bedtime Stories* and one set of the *Children's Hour*. While we ate lunch in the local café, he appeared restless.

"I think we had better go to Leduc where there are

many German people," he said. "You should do well there."

Less than an hour later we pulled up in front of a home in the country, south of Leduc. It was the residence of Clarence Goertzen, the local pastor. He and his wife had just finished eating their lunch and welcomed us cordially. After listening to Elder Spangler's plea on my behalf, the Goertzens invited me to stay with them and work the surrounding area.

"We have one spare bedroom, and you'll have to get used to our two little girls," they informed me. "We are a mile and a half off the pavement, so you'll have to walk a lot. If you don't mind that, you're welcome."

I didn't mind and was glad for such courtesy. Elder Spangler decided to drive to Millet, a small town about 15 miles south of Leduc, saying it would be just the right size for us to finish by suppertime. He worked until 5 p.m. and sold two more sets of children's books. Then he handed me the satchel containing the demonstration materials and order pads.

"It's all yours," he announced. "I've got to get back to Calgary."

Smiling, he got in his car, waved once more and was gone. The dust kicked up by his rear tires drifted gently back to earth. It suddenly dawned on me that I was now on my own. Several homes were left on the street we had been canvassing. With a silent prayer and heart pounding, I rang the doorbell of the closest home. A lady answered. I introduced myself as a student just over from Germany.

"Oh, you must come in. My husband and I are from the Netherlands. We haven't been here very long ourselves."

Calling her husband, who had been working outside, she offered me a seat. They had many questions relating to the situation in Europe and life behind the Iron Curtain. I tried answering as best I could. When they finally asked to see my books, I showed them the *Modern Medical Counselor* and *Desire of Ages*. After exchanging encouraging glances they ordered both books. I felt jubilant as I bade them goodbye and approached the next home. However, I made no more sales until I showed the *Bedtime Stories*, a three-volume set, to the lady occupying the last house on the block. She wanted only one book, which meant I had to split the set, something not recommended. She couldn't afford more, she told me. So I let her have the one she wanted.

It was now past 6 p.m. and time to get back to the Goertzens. It took me nearly an hour to hitchhike and walk another mile and a half. By the time I got there, they had finished their evening meal. However, Mrs. Goertzen fixed me something so I didn't have to go to bed hungry. I also met their two little girls, Lois (5) and Lila (3). They had been to a neighbor's home when Elder Spangler and I first visited.

Elder Goertzen was a tall slim man in his mid thirties with curly brown hair and horn-rimmed glasses. His wife, Alice, was of medium height with short, dark hair and wore clear-rimmed glasses. The girls were always very attentive during family worship, singing their Sabbath school songs with gusto and using pantomimes when their mother indicated. Alice was an excellent cook and I enjoyed the healthful food.

For nearly three weeks I worked the town of Leduc and vicinity, sometimes catching rides with Elder Goertzen, but mostly hitchhiking and walking. During the second week the Goertzens had to move. The house they were renting was being sold. I now slept on a couch in their living room in downtown Leduc.

On Sabbaths, I met the members of the Leduc church. Many had come into money when oil was discovered on their land. This caused them to erect a new church building five miles southwest of town on the road to Thorsby. It featured a full basement with children's classrooms, a spacious sanctuary seating 150 persons, balcony and baptistery. The congregation was made up mostly of Germans whose forefathers had come to Canada from Russia. Names such as Steinke, Wetter, Golz, Ratzlaff, Comm, Kruger, Kutzner, and Littman soon became familiar. All welcomed me and many invited me to their homes for meals. Their tables were always loaded with traditional German or Russian dishes. When they passed toothpicks around, I mistakenly tried chewing and swallowing them. I had never seen anything like it. "Now you'll get Dutch Elm disease," they teased. We had a good laugh.

The residents of Leduc among whom I called with my books also responded generously. Many wanted to talk about Germany and the situation there. I usually sold between two or three sets of children's books per day and other books as well. From Leduc, I moved on to Calmar, a small town on the road to Thorsby, and later to Thorsby itself. I attended a small church nearby on the weekends. August Comm, the church Elder, invited me to stay at his house south of Warburg. I spent the last week canvassing in that area.

At the end of my allotted six weeks, Elder Spangler confirmed my scholarship. I was free to enroll in the ministerial course at Canadian Union College with all lodging and tuition expenses covered for the entire school year. When I thanked him, he said, "You worked hard for it. We'll look forward to having you continue next summer."

"Next to God, you deserve all the credit," I insisted. "You steered me to territory that was receptive and church members who supported me all the way. I'll plan on next summer."

I shared my experiences with Mutti in a long letter. She responded by telling me that she had taken a trip to Westfalia to visit with her brother and sister. Apparently they had convinced her to leave Wallenfels and live near them. She was in the process of moving. "I don't know how I'm going to manage, but Uncle Willi promised to have a place for me when I get there and Aunt Grete thinks I won't have trouble finding a job. After reading about your new friends in Leduc, I would like to come to Canada myself," she wrote.

In my reply I cautioned, "Pray about that, and allow me time to see if we can find a sponsor. Without such a person there is no way."

Chapter
13

BACK ON CAMPUS

I soon adjusted to the routine of student life. Shortly after classes began, I met David Igler, a tall good-looking young man with penetrating dark eyes and straight black hair. He played the violin and was a good athlete and very popular with his peers.

He invited me to be his roommate and introduced me to his mother when she came to visit. I welcomed the opportunity to thank her personally for the package that brought so much joy to me. Modestly she told me, "It was a joint undertaking with the other Dorcas ladies. I'm glad the suit fit you."

By the end of the first semester, David and I realized that we were not compatible. He was an only child and so was I. We both were used to getting our own way! I moved in with Rudolph James, a black student from Trinidad, British West Indies. David's friendship with Orene Sahly eventually came to an end as well.

I had my eye on Ruby Bader, an attractive girl who, with her sister, worked as hostess in the dining room. She could speak German in the Swabian dialect. It charmed me. I invited her to a Saturday night travel-ogue. To my great pleasure, she accepted. However, it was to be our only date while we were students. She later became engaged to someone else. This setback caused me to devote all my attention to my studies.

The most difficult and time-consuming subject was English Rhetoric, taught by Roberta Moore, a hard taskmaster. When she rewarded my hard work with a "C," I was determined to show her that I could do better. The next year I earned a "B" in her Biblical Literature class, and the following year, an "A" in journalism, the highest grade.

Studying theology under Elders Gordon Balharrie, Ivan Crawford, and Hugh Campbell was both enjoyable and challenging. In a speech class taught by Elder Balharrie, I once mispronounced a word and expected immediate public censure. Instead of emphasizing the second "a" in catastrophe, I put the emphasis on the "o" which must have sounded very funny. To my amazement, nobody laughed or even snickered. Not until I finished my speech did our teacher correct my mistake, but he added, "I couldn't do as well in German as you do in English if our roles were reversed."

That attitude only further increased my admiration for him as a teacher and Christian gentleman. I was sorry when he left the campus before my final year to join the faculty of Walla Walla College, located in a little town called College Place, Washington.

During my first winter in Canada temperatures dropped to 40 degrees below zero. Walking from the dorm to the cafeteria for breakfast was truly a wake-up experience. Not equipped for this weather, I needed to find work to earn the funds for appropriate clothes. I secured a job digging a tunnel from the boiler room to Maple Hall that kept me below ground and from freezing.

Chapter
14

WORKING VACATIONS

The next summer my canvassing continued. This time the cities of Camrose and Wetaskiwin in central Alberta were assigned me. Fortunately, church members provided food and lodging. On Sabbath I joined a small company of believers who rotated through three homes, the Anderson home in Camrose, the Larsen home in New Norway, and the Clifford Johnson home in Gwynne. When there was no pastor, I substituted, sharing with these tolerant friends what I had learned in the classroom. They treated me kindly. I thank God for all of them, especially the Johnsons where I stayed while canvassing in Wetaskiwin. Getting to work required hitchhiking eight miles one way and then walking a mile to their farm on my return trip.

Toward the end of my second school year, I learned of a student looking for a companion to canvass in the Peace River country of northern Alberta. Doug Robertson owned his own car. This sounded exciting. We agreed to work together. He would take the countryside and I would work the towns. He would drop me off in the mornings and pick me up at night. We found an Adventist family near the little town of Nampa, 30 miles south of the town of Peace River. They agreed to let us stay in one of their empty granaries. We had to take care of our own food and bathe in a nearby river. Mosquitoes were huge and plentiful. Because the work went slowly, we often needed encouragement to go on. Doug would start singing and I would soon follow his lead. We remembered how the apostle Paul and his companion Silas sang in jail after they had been beaten. God saw us through.

Later we moved to Peoria on the Smoky River where, at that time, an active congregation worshipped in a spacious country church. The members, who were all farmers, welcomed and fed us, but insisted that we help them harvest their crops on Sunday. I learned what *stooking* meant. Freshly cut and bound sheaves of grain were stacked, like teepees, in the fields to dry. The hard work made my muscles sore by nightfall and glad to be canvassing again on Monday. One evening, a church member who owned a speedboat took us for a ride on the Smoky River. In this deserted country I saw my first wild bear and several moose. Before we returned to the college, I took my first driving lesson in a jeep owned by one of the farmers for whom we worked.

Once again we both received scholarships. Though our sales volume had gone down, the hours were up. This qualified us for more education. We were both grateful to God. For me this meant that I had earned my way through three years of college in Canada and the Lord had also provided for two years at Marienhoehe. There would be no debt hanging over my head after graduation.

During my senior year an Adventist couple, Henry Gimbel and his wife agreed to sponsor Mutti so that she could be present for my graduation. A generous couple, the Ivan Olsons from Leduc, provided funds for her ocean voyage and train ride to Lacombe. I shall always be grateful to them. The Gimbels, who had a home in the Rosedale Valley, just south of the college, promised Mutti lodging and food in return for house-keeping.

Chapter
15

MUTTI JOINS ME!

Mutti arrived at the Lacombe train station in the middle of April, 1956. She had been seasick during much of her ocean voyage and looked pale when we embraced after she disembarked, carrying the same suitcase we had tied to the back of her bicycle when we fled Haynau. What a joyous reunion! The Gimbels welcomed her like a member of their family. I visited frequently as the distance from the college was negligible.

She had much to tell me. Uncle Willi had visited her briefly in Wallenfels. He met a young widow, also from Silesia. The two had married and relocated to Westphalia, where he was again in the bakery business. After the Russians had killed his first wife, their little daughter was rescued and taken to West Germany. Later a little boy joined their family.

Aunt Grete had fled with all her children to Czechoslovakia, but never found her husband. Returning to Haynau, she spent almost a year under Russian occupation before Poland ordered all Germans out of their country. Aunt Grete then moved to East Germany where she found, providentially, her brother's address. He encouraged her to move to Westphalia so that they could live in close proximity to each other. Neither Uncle Willi nor Aunt Grete was in favor of Mutti coming to Canada, saying she would never adjust to her new environment nor learn to speak and read English, but Mutti felt she should go.

"What happened to Aunt Grete and the children under Russian occupation?" I asked curiously.

"Aunt Grete said that food was hard to come by. Her two boys had to beg from Russian soldiers. They had seen other German boys do that. To her surprise they brought home some bread. Not every day, however. They had learned the word *bread* in Russian and used it to their advantage. This, along with vegetables still available from their garden, helped them through."

"Did the soldiers ever molest any of the girls or Aunt Grete?" I asked.

"Not that she told me."

"How did she get from Czechoslovakia back to Haynau?"

"On foot, all the way, pulling a little wooden cart with whatever was left of their belongings."

"Do you remember anything else of interest?"

"Oh, something funny. Among the Russian soldiers were some from Mongolia. They had never seen light switches, ceiling lamps, water faucets, or flush toilets. They would stand in front of her kitchen sink turning the water on and off. One even tried to flush the toilet and clean potatoes in it. Still others wanted to take along the light switches and ceiling fixtures when they were ordered to move on. It took some convincing on Grete's part to dissuade them."

Mutti brought some pictures, among them one of the house her sister now lived in. The exterior qualified for a one-person dwelling. Yet, according to Mutti, Aunt Grete and her five children lived there in a kitchen, dining room/living room combination, and two bedrooms but no indoor toilet.

"Leave it to Aunt Grete to make do," I said admiringly, adding, "Whatever happened to the Steinerts and Edelgard?"

"To this day, I have not heard from any of them."

"How fortunate we were when you decided to go West instead of South to Czechoslovakia. God must have directed us. And now we are both together in Canada. Praise be to Him."

It was an answer to many prayers when in early June 1956, I was among the graduates marching into the crowded college auditorium to receive my Bachelor of Theology degree and later to be congratulated by my mother.

Chapter
16

PARISH MINISTRY

After a brief but largely unsuccessful canvassing experience in Mission City, British Columbia, I received a call to be pastor of the Medicine Hat district in southern Alberta. Mutti eventually joined me as my housekeeper since I was still single. My work demanded a lot of driving. In addition to the city church, I pastored the Hilda and Cassels congregations and a branch Sabbath school in Foremost. During my second year I joined the Chalmers-Friesen evangelistic team, then engaged in a six-month campaign in Calgary. Spending from Sunday to Thursday with the team, I took care of my district on weekends.

My 1949 Dodge, the first automobile I ever owned, got quite a workout. I had financed its entire cost of $550 with the help of Conference officials. On its maiden voyage to Lacombe, it stalled in a busy intersection in downtown Calgary. Amid the blaring horns of irritated motorists, I secured assistance from a nearby service station. The gentleman slipped behind the steering wheel, turned the key, and then shouted above the noise, "What's the matter? Your car is running!"

But there were compensations. I learned much about soul winning from Elder Chalmers, a seasoned evangelist, whom I accompanied on visits to the homes of interested persons. Jerry Friesen, a gifted vocalist, allowed me to sleep in the basement of his home and enjoy the hospitality of his wife and the antics of their little daughter.

A baptismal class followed the evening presentations. Among those attending regularly were two young ladies, sisters. One was married and the other, Donna, was still single and quite attractive. The Chalmers' arranged for us to meet over a meal in their home. This marked the beginning of a courtship that lasted almost a year. Donna and I became engaged. She visited in Medicine Hat and met Mutti. Things were going well until she accepted an offer to work at our denomination's Rest Haven Hospital on Vancouver Island. Several months later she wrote to dissolve our engagement. I was devastated. "Dear God," I prayed frequently, "Please help me find the right girl."

During the Christmas season of 1957, Ruby Bader, whose parents were members of the Medicine Hat church, came to spend the holidays at home. The spark that she had ignited in me when I escorted her to the travelogue three years prior, had never been fully extinguished. Discovering from her parents that her engagement had also been dissolved, I asked her to be part of a singing band that solicited funds for the less fortunate. She accepted and we had a wonderful evening. One afternoon she agreed to accompany me on a trip to the country, even forgiving me when we hit a patch of ice and landed in a ditch. Before she returned to Portland for the last five months of her nurse's training, she agreed to marry me. We both felt God had planned this union all along.

Our wedding took place in the Medicine Hat church on June 16, 1958. Besides Mutti and Ruby's large family, guests included Ernest Farnsworth, the head elder of the Cassels church that was part of my district. In his early nineties and in excellent health, he was the last of the 22 children of William Farnsworth, who in Washington, New Hampshire, had been part of the first congregation of Adventists to observe the seventh-day Sabbath.

For the next six years we worked in three Alberta districts. After Medicine Hat, we served the Leduc and Thorsby churches and the New Norway Company. While living in Wetaskiwin our son Mark was born on June 13, 1959. These congregations were made up of the same people I had met while canvassing. It was a mixed blessing, as most of these dear people saw me as one of them rather than an authority figure. We decided to work for the young people, organizing Pathfinder Clubs and training youth to participate in public evangelism. Some of our clubs consisted of non-church members. Before we left that area, several young people with no previous religious affiliation joined our church, dissipating the initial skepticism of some of the older church members. When we held an investiture service at the Leduc church, three clubs participated, filling the sanctuary with parents, counselors, and visitors.

Our next district included the Stettler, Sedgewick, Loyalist, and Hanna churches. In addition we started a branch Sabbath school in Oyen. This meant that we sometimes traveled 250 miles on a single Sabbath. Our second son, Tim, joined our family on Mother's Day, March 14, 1961. Ruby often said that our boys were practically born in a car since we had to be on the road so much. To drive 45,000 miles in a year was considered average.

Most of our church members were quite self-sufficient. When the Stettler congregation decided to operate a church school and wondered how to finance it, Art Kay and Bill Wigley, both elders, came up with a unique solution. Art, a cattle rancher, proposed that each willing member who owned a farm buy a calf in the spring and feed it till late fall. Bill, an auctioneer, would supervise the selling of these animals when they were at the proper weight. The idea caught on, thus doubling and in some cases tripling the initial investment. Tuition costs for all students were thus covered.

The Sedgewick church also exhibited a high degree of creativity. Members of the Anderson family, hearty Scandinavians, made up the bulk of that congregation. Five brothers farmed and worked well together. They had provided most of the funds and labor for their new sanctuary. Somehow they always arranged to have an Adventist teacher in the nearby public school that their children attended. When I suggested we start a radio program, I received an enthusiastic response. With so much local talent, it was a success from the beginning. Harry Anderson, a gifted local soloist, contributed generously. We also managed to get the *Voice of Prophecy* program on a radio station in Camrose, paid for by the Sedgewick and Wetaskiwin members.

During the Lacombe camp meeting in June of 1960, five candidates were ordained to the gospel ministry, I among them. President Walter Nelson of the Canadian Union of Seventh-Day Adventists presided.

From the Summer of 1962 to the Fall of 1963, we lived in Ponoka, where Ruby practiced her nursing skills at the Provincial Mental Hospital, while I tried to improve my writing skills. Ever since completing my journalism course under Roberta Moore, I longed for an opportunity to serve the church in a public relations capacity. In the summer of 1963, I attended a Writer's Conference convened on the campus of Columbia Union College, near Washington DC. There I met Don Roth and Cecil Coffey, public relation secretaries for the Columbia and Southern Union respectively. Both encouraged me to come to the United States and promised to keep their eyes and ears open for employment opportunities.

Less than a month later I received an invitation from the administrator of the new C.F. Kettering Memorial Hospital in Dayton, Ohio, to connect with that institution as director of public relations.

Ruby, our boys, and I arrived there during the last week of September. Mutti joined us three months later. My dream of living in the United States of America, sparked by my grandmother when I was a little boy, had finally come true.

Chapter
17

CHAPLAINCY

For the next 30 years we worked in the United States, the first five at the new Kettering Memorial Hospital in Ohio. During the dedication ceremony on Sunday, February 16, 1964, Dr. Edward Annis, then President of the American Medical Association, addressed a vast audience of prominent citizens including the Kettering family and their friends, medical staff, and employees. Church leadership was represented by R. R. Figuhr, President of the General Conference; Francis D. Nichol, Editor of the *Review and Herald*; and Neal Wilson, North American Division President. Don Roth spent the entire weekend with me, teaching me to work with the various news media. His periodic visits over the next six months always encouraged me, and I will remain forever grateful to him.

After a year, it became evident that I would not be able to continue without experienced help. George Nelson, administrator of the hospital, agreed and called Norman Squehler, a veteran public relations man from

Southern California, to head the department. I was given the opportunity to split my time between two departments, public relations and chaplaincy.

"Give yourself six months and then decide which direction you want to proceed," said Nelson.

Albert Brendel, Director of the Pastoral Care Department, made it easy to decide. He was even-tempered, patient, genuinely caring while he instructed me in bedside ministry, clergy education, and eventually how to conduct the Five Day Plan to Stop Smoking. Watching Elman Folkenberg and J. Wayne McFarland, MD, the originators of the program, and Ellsworth Wareham, a surgeon from Loma Linda, conduct five sessions in our large hospital auditorium convinced me that I must get involved. There were more than 600 participants. We organized follow-up in the form of weekly fitness classes under direction of a popular YMCA instructor. This earned us excellent publicity and demand for more programs throughout the year.

While Albert took the lead during the first year, he eventually turned the program over to me. In addition to the evening sessions, we began visiting elementary and secondary schools in our area. Two pathologists, Erlo Roth and Glenn Bylsma, agreed to help. We used the film, *One in Twenty Thousand*, which showed the removal of a cancerous lung to stimulate our young audiences. Afterwards, the pathologists displayed samples of smoke-damaged tissue and answered questions. It proved popular, and invitations came from distant schools.

I thoroughly enjoyed my work but was concerned about the long-range success of those who stopped smoking. Statistical studies revealed that many smokers return to their habit three to six months after quitting. I wondered if a controlled environment, away from the stress of work and family might improve the odds. But where could such a place be found? The answer was in California.

Chapter
18

WE MOVE TO CALIFORNIA

I had heard of the St. Helena Hospital in Northern California that had added a hotel-like building for people from the Bay area who periodically came for rest and relaxation, while also getting medical checkups. It sounded like the right place for smokers going through withdrawal pains.

When a chaplain's position became vacant, I applied and was accepted. Our family, including Mutti, arrived on Labor Day of 1968. By now Mark had completed two grades in elementary school and Tim was ready for first grade. Ruby had been a part-time surgical nurse for most of the five years we worked in Kettering. Trained to give back rubs to patients and to pray with them at night, she was glad to hear that nurses at St. Helena carried on this tradition. She agreed to continue working part time, on the evening shift. Mutti was our built-in baby-sitter. We found a rental two blocks from Elmshaven, the last home of Ellen White.

With the support of Charles Snyder, the administrator, and the help of a small committee, we designed a seven-day residential stop-smoking program that was launched the following April. As far as I know, it was the first of its kind in the United States.

While our success was moderate at first, steady improvements followed after Alan Rice, a recent graduate of the Loma Linda School of Public Health joined us. The length of the program was reduced to five days and offered twice and sometimes three times per month. By 1974, Ann Landers had taken note and sent her husband and daughter, both smokers. She wrote of it in her syndicated column, resulting in 3,000 inquiries within a week. An independent study conducted under a Government grant determined that our program enjoyed a 45 percent success ratio over one year. The national average for non-residential programs was then about 15-18 percent.

One of my duties as hospital chaplain included visiting and conducting worships at the nearby Crystal Springs residence for retirees. Among those enjoying their golden years was Elder Ernest Lloyd, former editor of *Our Little Friend*. He had been an errand boy at Michigan's famous Battle Creek Sanitarium and had some fascinating stories to share. He agreed to have me interview him in front of the guests that came to stop smoking. He also served as tour guide through Elmshaven where we took our guests before proceeding to the Robert Louis Stevenson museum in downtown St. Helena.

Elder Lloyd, then in his 90's, modeled health reform convincingly and was admired for his excellent memory and quick wit. He recalled meeting some prominent people while he worked at the Sanitarium including William Jennings Bryan, Thomas Edison and wife, Henry Ford, Harvey Firestone, and John D. Rockefeller. Rockefeller offered Dr. Kellogg, head of the Sanitarium, a million dollars for a new stomach, Lloyd recalled, but the doctor couldn't comply. They didn't transplant organs in those days. Instead, he prescribed 20 rules for the millionaire to follow daily. Apparently, Rockefeller took them to heart. He lived to be 98!

Lloyd also recalled being in the Battle Creek Physical Therapy Department when President William Howard Taft stepped on the scales, which tipped at nearly 300 pounds. Turning to the attendants, the President was overheard saying, "Do your best boys."

Here is the story of corn flakes as told by Lloyd. "Mrs. J.H. Kellogg was a nutritionist, always experimenting in her kitchen to come up with new recipes. One day her rolling pin, which she used for baking, accidentally dropped into a boiling kettle of wheat. She needed it quickly so stuck it in the oven to dry. When she pulled it out shortly thereafter, she scraped off the baked-on wheat. It looked like something her husband might want to taste, which he did later on that evening saying, 'This is it!' Thus, when corn was later substituted for wheat, the idea of *corn flakes* was born. However, it was W. K. Kellogg, John Harvey's half-brother, who transformed this idea into a thriving industry. He became known as the 'Cornflake King.'"

Asked to share the secret of his long and happy life, Lloyd would explain it this way: "I've always been a light eater, have never weighed more than 130 pounds. Three light meals a day and NEVER a bite between. NO SECOND helping of dessert! The vegetarian program is the best for the human body." Then, raising his voice he intoned: "Avoid sugar. This country is cursed with too much of it." Next he zeroed in on the digestive system: The most important canal is not the Suez, but your alimentary canal. Eat yoghurt, it's good for you, but take the plain kind!"

He practiced what he preached. I often saw him in the hospital cafeteria, finishing his meal with a generous serving of yoghurt, plain. He walked from his 2nd floor apartment at the Crystal Springs Manor to the cafeteria for his daily meals down and then up a steep trail. "I try not to use the elevator. Walking up the stairs is good for your heart!" When we moved away from St. Helena he was 98 years old. Seven years later he passed away, at age 105.

Elder Lloyd never failed to credit Ellen White for influencing Dr. Kellogg and his wife and for laying the foundation of Adventist Health Reform. It was my goal to expose all Health Center guests to this material. With help from Arthur White, Ellen's grandson, we put together a six-page pamphlet and made it available to all the guests visiting Elmshaven.

During the almost eleven years we spent working at the St. Helena Hospital and Health Center, I continued my involvement with the Stop Smoking program except for the final three years. Early on, Alan Rice with assistance from Terry Hansen and Treva Burgess, organized his own department. He had a number of physicians helping, including Harold James, Lester Rose, Duane Brueske, Herschel Lamp, and Clarence Eckvall. Beside the Lloyd interviews, I shared equal time with the physicians during the evening lectures, and also facilitated group therapy sessions.

Spiritual components of the program included prayers before dinner in the formal dining room, midday chapel services, and a Wednesday night information session for those inquiring about Adventist beliefs. Response to these efforts were often expressed in letters received in the chaplain's office. Here are just three samples. (There were many more)

> I am so grateful to God for sending me to St. Helena, first, to stop the horrible smoking habit (which I could not do alone), and second, for permitting me to observe the Christian way of life as lived by Seventh-day Adventists. As a Catholic, I have great respect for all of you at St. Helena and actually feel some bit of envy in the things you stand for.—Tom V., Louisiana

I doubt that you will ever know how grateful I am for your re-acquainting me with the power of prayer and your prescription for a more spiritual life.—Alice S., San Ramon, CA

I enjoyed your tiny chapel. I have visited many of the great cathedrals of the world. They provide vast space and awe; your chamber attends compactness and intimacy with God. I glimpsed again the beauty of simplicity of the Christian faith. I'm finished with cigarettes...for good.—Charles H., Palo Alto, CA

Thursday afternoon hikes to the Stevenson Monument on the slopes of Mt. St. Helena provided opportunities to get better acquainted with program participants. On one of these hikes I met a former B-17 pilot who had dropped bombs on Chemnitz, Germany, the site of the air raid during which Mutti and I barely escaped from that badly damaged railroad car.

It was my privilege to preside at Friday morning "graduation exercises" when participants signed pledge cards as reminders to "choose" not to smoke. To fortify their choice, a prayer for divine help and protection on their homeward journey concluded the program. A first-person account of one of the "graduates" is reprinted in the next chapter.

★ ★ ★

During this time the American Protestant Hospital Association strongly recommended that chaplains be certified by their organization. Clarence Miller, my Adminstrator, allowed me to take the required four quarters of Clinical Pastoral Education. Fortunately, I was able to complete three quarters at Napa State Hospital, an easy 18 mile commute from St. Helena, while still carrying out most of my regular duties. The final quarter, taken at Loma Linda University Medical Center in southern California, proved to be the most challenging. However, my efforts were rewarded in the spring of 1976 when I was among a small group of chaplains certified as a Fellow of the College of Chaplains during the APHA convention in Cincinnati, Ohio.

When no longer needed for the Stop Smoking programs, I began spending a day each week in Lake County, 60 miles north of St. Helena, visiting newly discharged patients who had undergone coronary by-pass surgery in our facility. Those who had welcomed my bedside ministry now opened their homes to me. When they voiced spiritual concerns, I introduced them to pastors of the three Adventist churches in Lake County. Some former patients attended Sabbath morning services during my visits.

None of these activities would have been possible without the support of my office staff. Bertha Parmentier, "Parmy," for short, then already in her 70's, worked like someone half her age. Betty Brophy, a Bible Instructor, visited former patients tirelessly in the community. She had people ready for baptism every year. David Gramlich, confined to a wheel chair because of multiple sclerosis, also assisted me, as did Duane Grimstad, pastor of the nearby Sanitarium Church. His help was especially vital while I was at Loma Linda taking CPE. I owe a great deal of gratitude to all these people.

Meanwhile Ruby had joined the staff of the newly opened psychiatric unit on the third floor of the hospital. Mutti worked in the hospital's housekeeping department. Our boys were growing up fast and both enrolled in nearby denominational schools. We purchased a three-bedroom home on a hillside overlooking the Napa Valley. During vacations our family explored Yosemite National Park and Mt. Shasta, sleeping in a VW camper we had brought back from Germany where Ruby and I visited in the Fall of 1968. These were truly the best years of my life.

Nothing this good can last forever. God knows how to keep me humble. Mutti, having retired after turning 65, moved into her own apartment next to the hospital. Two months later she was diagnosed with cancer of the pancreas. This came as quite a shock to us. She had lived a very active life, was careful in her health habits, and had practiced vegetarianism long before we became Adventists. Just when she should be enjoying retirement, she became terminally ill.

Ruby and I offered many a sincere prayer for God to spare her life. We called the elders of our church, following the Biblical instructions in James 5:15. They anointed her with oil and prayed that she might be healed. While her spirits were lifted and she found peace in her heart, her body continued to deteriorate. It was hard to see her shriveling from a healthy 140 pounds to less than 90 pounds in just six months and battling almost continuous pain. Despite many a prayer, there was no miracle.

She loved her little apartment. I visited her often. Once I found her sitting near the window overlooking the Napa Valley, an open Bible on her lap. She had a far-away look in her eyes and surprised me with her optimism as she shared her feelings.

"I'm so glad the Lord allowed me to live with you and Ruby for nine years. I had so much fun watching Mark and Tim grow up. God provided employment for me in the hospital where you work, so we could see each other often. Now He has given me this lovely apartment with such a grand view and good friends who drop by to see me. Why should I complain? Best of all, Jesus is preparing a place for all of us. Someday, we will all be together again!"

When I hugged her, my eyes were moist. Hers were

clear, reflecting a child-like trust and submission to God's will.

In early April of 1974, she was admitted to the hospital. We knew the end was near. A few days later, early one morning shortly after 4 a.m., we were called to her bedside. She was very uncomfortable, but conscious. While the nurse went to get another injection ready, Ruby and I linked hands while I placed my other hand upon Mutti's shoulder as we prayed once more, asking God to ease her suffering. This time He heard us. Shortly after she had received the injection, she breathed her last.

We tiptoed from the room, shaken, yet grateful that her struggles were over. She had "fought the good fight," and kept the faith. God would surely reward her accordingly.

Unfortunately, Uncle Willi and Aunt Grete could not attend her funeral. Financial considerations and distance made it impossible. Shortly after Mutti was informed concerning her future, I made a tape recording, which expressed her faith and also urged her brother and sister to make their peace with God before their end approached. On my next trip to Germany I was able to play this recording for both of them.

Mutti is buried at the St. Helena cemetery, near the grave of Elder J.N. Loughborough, one of the staunch pioneers who introduced Adventism to California.

The author stepping into a New World—at the Montreal airport—August 16, 1953

Top left: Ernest Lloyd, pastor, administrator, editor, tour guide; at one time bell-boy to the Kelloggs of Battle Creek, Michigan, shared his secrets of longevity with Health Center guests during Stop Smoking programs. He died at age 105.

Top right: Ernest E. — son of William Farnsworth of Washington, New Hampshire, seen here weeding his garden at 96 years of age. He attended our wedding.

Bottom: St. Helena Hospital and Health Center, in the Napa Valley of California, where guests came from far and near to stop smoking.

Mutti with the Müllers and Hans Zuber in Wallenfels, enjoying nature. From left: Brigitte Müller, Mutti, Christa Müller, her mother (Elfriede) and Hans.

Our family at St. Helena, California: Dieter, Ruby, Mark, Tim.

500th Smoker Registers for Help at St. Helena Health Center

Smoker number 500 registered at the St. Helena Hospital and Health Center last week to seek education for a way of life without tobacco. She was Polly Aldigé of Woodside, a smoker for the last 33 years.

Since its inception during 1969 by Chaplain Dieter Hain, would-be ex-smokers have traveled to the live-in, controlled-environment program from 20 states outside of California and Mexico. They represent Americans from the East Coast to the Hawaiian Islands.

A government-funded study in Pennsylvania has revealed from meticulous records kept by St. Helena Volunteer Vera Schmidt that 40% of the graduates had not smoked after a year. This percentage far excells any other program studied, according to Health Educator Alan J. Rice.

Such successes belong to God Himself, the One honored in lectures by the medical staff and in the lives of hospital personnel. Ellen White wrote in 1904 that the religious influence pervading our institutions inspires the guests with confidence. (CH 208)

St. Helena is proving that to be true in 1972.

Thirty-three-year smoker Polly Aldige of Woodside, California gave a pack of cigarettes to Administrator Clarence Miller in exchange for the volume, Life at its Best.

Reprinted from *Pacific Union Recorder*

ann landers

Dear Ann Landers: You have printed several letters in your column about smokers, how they hate the habit and wish they could get unhooked, but never have you printed a letter with a solution. This may be your first.

I started to smoke when I was 17. I was on my own in the business world and thought if I smoked I'd look older. For a few years it was eight or 10 cigarettes a day, usually when I was with someone I wanted to impress.

Gradually I realized I was smoking more than I had intended. I found myself lighting a cigarette every time I had a cup of coffee, or whenever I reached for a telephone. By the time I was 21, I was hooked.

I coughed, hacked, and burned holes in my best suits. I even burned a hole in the dining room table. I must say my wife was wonderful. She never nagged me to quit because she was smart enough to know that each person must make that decision himself.

Last November some friends from Reno came to spend the weekend. Edna mentioned something about an acquaintance who had been a nicotine freak for 38 years, how she had gone to a clinic in California, checked in on Sunday and left the following Friday — total cost, $375.

Edna said that woman was a chain-smoker, thoroughly addicted, but five days at "that place" produced the miracle. I sent for the literature at once.

On Dec. 2, I left for St. Helena's Hospital and Health Center. When I arrived at the gate I was smoking. Then I saw a sign, "You are entering a non-smoking area. Deposit smoking materials here." I put out my cigarette and tossed it (along with the rest of the pack) into the trash can provided for that purpose.

The next five days were rough, but they were fascinating, too. I met men and women

Clinic cures chain smoker

from all over the country. We exercised vigorously, ate vegetarian meals, drank countless glasses of fruit juice (no liquor allowed), listened to lectures, watched films, and took steam and sauna baths to ease the withdrawal symptoms.

Then there was "Frank," that horrible-looking, cancer-ridden lung floating in a bottle of alcohol. He managed to turn up in the dining room, the lecture hall, wherever I happened to be.

Although St. Helena's is run by the Seventh Day Adventists, no one tried to sell us religion. I was impressed by the quiet dignity of the personnel. They truly believe in what they are doing but they apply no pressure to persuade the guests that theirs is the only way.

On Friday, Dec. 7, I walked out of St. Helena's feeling very good about myself. "Keep in touch," said Dr. Herschel Lamp, the director. "We want to know how you get along." From that day to this I haven't had a cigarette. Easy? Of course

not! There are times when the craving is so strong I must excuse myself from a meeting and go wash my face with cold water. (They taught us to do this during moments of crisis.)

But I have kicked the habit, Honey, and if I can do it, anyone can.

Please print this letter and tell the tobacco junkies who want to quit where to write for information. Thank you.— FREE AT LAST

Dear Free: The address is: St. Helena's Hospital and Health Center, Deer Park, Calif. 94576. All I can say is God bless THEM and thank you for writing.

A no-nonsenese approach to how to deal with life's most difficult and most rewarding arrangement. Ann Landers' booklet, "Marriage — What to Expect," will prepare you for better or worse. Send your request to Ann Landers, P.O. Box 3346, Chicago, Ill. 60654, enclosing 50 cents in coin and a long, stamped, self-addressed envelope.

Marienhoehe Seminary, in Germany, near Darmstadt.
(*Review & Herald* photo)

Canadian Union College (now Canadian University College) in Alberta. Administration Building.
(Photo by the author)

Chapter
19

FIVE DAYS TO FREEDOM*
by
Bernice B. Carton

It was D-day minus one. I couldn't sleep. My own private countdown had begun – and I was scared. Something made me get out of bed, make a cup of coffee, and have a cigarette – or two. There won't be many more. Only one more day to smoke. Tomorrow they're taking away the only good thing in my life.

Whoa! Nobody's taking anything away. I made the decision. I was tired of being a slave to a habit I had long ago decided was dirty, smelly, and unhealthy. All that will be taken away is the bad breath that I'm self-conscious about, and the nagging fear of what I'm doing to destroy myself. And it's not going to be taken away! I have to do it all by myself.

OOPS. Not quite. I haven't been able to make it all by myself. That's how I happened to get into this group situation and this ridiculous, middle-of-the-night panic. Quick! Light up another, D-day is closer.

The decision had been a long time in coming. The

---

* Reprinted from *Smoke Signals*: Dec. 1972 Vol. XVIII No. 12

immediate cause was the uninviting-looking brochure sent by a well-meaning friend. The accompanying note said tersely, "It worked for me. Why don't you give it a try?"

I read the brochure then and laughed. "FIVE DAYS TO FREEDOM. STOP SMOKING THROUGH THE SAINT HELENA PLAN. A THREE-PHASED AT-TACK," the brochure read. "MOTIVATIONAL, EDU-CATIONAL." Lectures! "PHYSICAL." Physical therapy! Exercise! Were they serious about getting people out before breakfast for calisthenics and hikes? A hearty HO! HO! Breakfast is a cup of coffee and cig... oh dear.

There was one interesting note in the brochure. That bit about "contagious interaction of a group determined to kick the habit together." Now there was something. If only I had the company that misery craves while I was battling the first few days.

"You crazy, or something?" people asked. "Going all the way to California?" But it was the only place I knew where, for five days each month, up to 20 would-be non-smokers participated in a live-in situation.

My teen-age son looked at me with some amusement. "First time I've sent my mom to camp," he chuckled. "Want me to mail cookies?"

SUNDAY AFTERNOON:

A kind friend, who sent the brochure, drove very slowly from San Francisco to St. Helena to allow time for one more cigarette, before the moment.

The butterflies still had me, but I was determined. Once again this morning the operator addressed me on the phone as "Sir." That cut it. If for no other reason than the hope of sounding less hoarse and reasonably female on the phone, I'll stick with this decision.

"Here we are," my friend said. "Want another cigarette?"

I knew perfectly well that in an hour I'd want one desperately. But just now, after the hysterical smoking I'd done on the drive up, I couldn't possibly stand even one more puff.

The Napa Valley was beautiful and the St. Helena Health Center that was perched on the side of a hill commanded a delightful view. Bravely I left the cigarettes in my friend's car. Except that, when she wasn't looking, I filched one cigarette and hid it in my purse. I felt wicked. Later I found that half my non-smoking group had done the same.

Registration in the lobby combined the features of coming into a deluxe hotel, with overtones of college dormitory and only the faintest tinges of hospital. I was given a packet with information and scheduled *guest activities*.

1:00 P.M.

Buffet lunch. But, hey now! My friend neglected to mention one little item! This place is vegetarian. And to cap off the horror, they don't serve coffee or tea. Can I survive! I was told that adherence to a vegetarian diet and abstinence from ??? seemed helpful in reducing the craving for nicotine.

Lunch turned out to be not so bad after all. There was an array of hot dishes and cold. Lima beans, squash, tomatoes, baked potatoes, a wide variety of salads, homemade biscuits and a drink of a vaguely lavender hue, which turned out to be lavender-colored lemonade. Lots of fruit juices were set out.

My no-smoke colleagues hadn't yet arrived. I sat at the table with Alan Rice, health education director for the center. Surprisingly young for so responsible a job, he likes to expound on the subject of preventive medicine. I'd hear a lot more about this, I suspected, since the heath center was founded on the precepts of preventive medicine.

After lunch I was called in for a physical checkup, since I'd neglected to bring my own physician's form, the examining doctor asked a few questions about my state of health. But mostly it was a dissertation on the benefits of exercise. I mumbled that I couldn't abide exercise.

I suspected that he found my attitude deplorable. Nevertheless, my heart and lungs were apparently present and accounted for. The doctor scribbled something and I was in.

Back in my own room, I started to sneak that last cigarette. I wondered insanely if *they* had spies stationed near roof ventilators to sniff out smoking cheats. Would they kick me out? In a wild attempt to rid the room of the giveaway odor, I opened the sliding glass doors to the balcony and flapped my arms madly to dissipate the smoke.

Then I decided that was nonsense. I also decided it was nonsense to come all this way to kick the habit and then sneak behind the bathroom doors to smoke. I started to crush out the butt, then impulsively clinched it, wrapped it, and stowed it at the bottom of my cosmetic bag. I rationalized that it was insurance against going into a nicotine withdrawal coma.

4:30 P.M.

The guest activities sheet indicated that the program was scheduled to start with an orientation followed by a tour of the health center. So we met in the parlor. There were eight of us altogether, five men and three women, one of which was a non live-in from a nearby town who came just for the evening sessions. Everybody introduced himself or herself. This suddenly took on a strangely gay air. We were a bunch of kids at boarding school or camp, a feeling of unexpected holiday. Maybe my teen-age son was closer to the truth than I thought. Just possibly this whole five days might turn out to be less repulsive than I feared.

Chaplain Hain, a cheerful, youngish gentleman with a merry smile and an equally glowing tie, greeted us. Everybody here was genuinely cheerful. The cheeriness was contagious.

We were shown around the health center and introduced to dietitians, hobby lady, librarian, physical therapists, and a hearty scoutmaster-type that turned out to be Jerry King, in charge of those early morning calisthenics and hikes, and a very important member of the team. "Just call me Jerry, the deep-breath king." His enthusiasm proved infectious, and while we were busy laughing, we were also busy exercising. If I wasn't careful, I'd end up trapped in this exercise bit.

6:00 P.M.

Dinner time. The eight of us sat at two tables for four. We were a pretty mixed bag, but tied with a thread of mutual need and interest. Everyone looked pleasant and friendly. Some looked as if they felt foolish, some were scared, and some defiant of themselves.

Mary Ann was probably in her fifties, a big woman but warm and direct. She was a schoolteacher. I got the feeling that her pupils liked and respected her. She liked them as well in a no-nonsense kind of way.

"It's these first five days that worry me," Mary Ann said. "I live alone and every now and then I get to feeling sorry for myself. Then I start to feel that cigarette is my only friend."

She looked at Howard encouragingly, not wanting to infringe upon his privacy. If you talk here you'll never lack for an interested audience. Say nothing and no one will question. But Howard wanted to talk.

"I go to AA meetings," he volunteered. "See I'm an ex-drunk. Been off the stuff for nine years. But at these meetings there's a lot of smoking, and I guess I'll just have to stay away from them for awhile. Anyhow, I got religious reasons for stopping." Everyone stared at him, puzzled.

"Religious?" asked Mac hoarsely and then went into a spasm of coughing. This was the first time Mac had said anything. I figured him for maybe sixty, but because he was pale and unhealthy, I could be off in my estimate. He seemed so embarrassed by his coughing fit that I began to understand why he talked so little. Mac had emphysema. And still, he was a two-pack-a-day man. He's a dead man if he doesn't quit right now.

"Yep," Howard answered. "I got religious reasons. See, I figure it this way. One of these days I'm going to have to face them up there and account for, well, I figure my body is a tabernacle, a temple. It was given to me. And, well, I haven't been doing such a good job of taking care of it. And when I have to answer for why I treated it so bad, well, you see what I mean. So I figure on this being my last chance to make it. I'm sure gonna give it a try."

Jeanette sighed, "I wish I had your reasons, Howard. A stronger motivation would make it a little easier for me." She didn't look at Mac, but she and Mary Ann exchanged brief, sympathetic glances. Here we barely knew each other and already something of the atmosphere of this place was beginning to get to everyone. We were starting to feel a little responsibility for each other.

Jeanette went on, "Oh, I know intellectually it's not good for me. I guess what's really bothering me, is that I don't like to be all that dependent on something. I just feel that I've got to quit. I'm tired of being a slave to a stupid habit."

Jeanette was a legal translator with a large weight of responsibility in her career. She was the sort of woman who was used to giving orders and instructions to others and resented her own inability to give them to herself.

"Hey!" Jim bellowed from the other table. "You know what we got here? We got us a guy we're here to outsmart." He reached around to smack his neighbor on the shoulder in a friendly fashion. "We got Digger O'Dell, your friendly undertaker. His real name's Perry. Haw, haw, haw!" Everyone was old enough to remember the radio character.

Perry beamed at the group through his horn-rimmed bifocals. "Don't worry," he said reassuringly. "You all look great. Except maybe him. You look a little pale, Jim, Haw, haw!" Perry the *merry mortician*! "What's the matter, Jim? Not enough fruit juice?"

"Fruit juice! Boy, they sure have a thing here for fruit juice. I've drunk enough fruit juice, and pure spring water, to float my brain out the front door." Said Jim shuddering. "Remember? They showed us the juice bar on the second floor. Said we were to guzzle whenever we think of it, or get lonely, or want a smoke."

I remembered. That was the place to go when the night willies got me. There was always a cheerful nurse or aid there to talk to, kid around with, or to drink juice with.

Jim winked at John, the fourth at his table, "Saw a real cutie up there near the juice bar. Think I'll get a nicotine fit tonight when you guys are all safely tucked away."

John grinned back at him, glad to be mistaken for a hell-raiser. John was away from his wife and children and retail shop for the first time in his life. He felt he was raising teen-agers in troubled times. And while there was little he could do to help them, he could, at least, set a good example. He would kick the smoking thing. John was a good husband and a responsible parent.

7:00 P.M.

Every night there was a medical lecture in the parlor. Tonight it was one of the heath center's cardiologists speaking on coronary disease and its prevention. The lectures were attended not only by the Stop Smoking people, but also by any of the heart disease prevention patients who wanted to come.

7:50 P.M.

Break time. Everyone was encouraged to go for a brisk stroll about the grounds to get the old circulation going again. Those who didn't want to walk settled for several stretches and gobs of deep breathing. This breathing bit was big stuff around here. That and exercise, oh, and lets not forget about the fruit juice. Well, if I couldn't have a lung full of cigarette smoke, I might as well see what happened when I filled up on clean air.

8:15 P.M.

Parlor again. I was still sleepy, but my circulation was going again. This is the time that belonged exclusively to the quitters. Every night the St. Helena Five-day Plan to Stop Smoking unfolded under the auspices of the staff. Tonight, it was Chaplain Hain who began. I was surprised at how simple some of the things were.

One of the simplest was also one of the most helpful. The longest craving for a smoke, over-powering as it seemed, would never last more than three minutes. I could look at my watch and say, "I CHOOSE not to smoke for thirty seconds," I could be certain that the most I would have to repeat this choice only five times, and then the craving would have dissipated.

That this was a personal choice is important. Chaplain Hain drove a most insistent point here. Were it a promise, albeit a promise to yourself, should you ever break it, it would be bad business psychologically, but because it is a choice, it leads to a happier psychological situation.

A buddy system was instituted this first night to help lend strength in this struggle against Ol' Debbil smoke. Buddy would come in handy, too, if I fell asleep again in any of the lectures. He could fill me in on what I missed. Provided, of course, he stayed awake.

Literature was handed out. Buddy poked me. Apparently, I fell asleep. I missed the part about drinking lots of water and juice in an all-out attempt to bathe my nicotine-coated innards. I wondered if this water and juice thing had a valid scientific basis, or was it just a gimmick to take my mind off smoking?

MONDAY, 6:30 A.M.

"Good morning," the cheery voice on the phone bubbled. "It's time to get ready for sunrise calisthenics. Don't forget to stop on two for your juice."

I was shocked to find myself leaping out of bed, actually looking forward to juice time. Was I losing my mind to be able to face the day without the grumps? And was I really going to join the gang for exercise? Calisthenics at sunrise, indeed?

The team gathered in the juice room. Sleep information was exchanged. At seven on the dot, Jerry the Deep-breath king bounced in, accompanied by Flanagan. I wondered who she was. Flanagan, who preferred not to have a first name, was a small bundle of irrepressible energy topped by a big grin. She's a nurse who loves to join the exercise group, particularly at sunup. She admitted to being sixty-five and had just finished her midnight stint, Jerry referred to it as the graveyard shift. Jim reproached him. "Watch your language, pal."

Flanagan was ready to relax with half an hour or so of vigorous calisthenics to tone her up before beginning her normal daytime activities of weeding her garden and chopping down trees. She pulled on her worn brown mittens, shrugged her dusty-rose sweater into place over the top of her too-long white uniform that flapped around her calves, and trotted happily in place, bursting with impatience to get started. Apparently, she had no need for sleep. This first morning, Flanagan was a bit formidable. Nobody can possibly have all that much energy and good cheer, can they?

"Let's polish up those arteries!" Jerry cried. And I got the sinking sensation that I was going to end up doing just that. Nobody's making me participate. Not a soul here to twist my arm. And look! Here I go up to the roof, to polish up arteries!

After all the trotting, jogging, stretching, and bending, Jerry the Breather had a surprise. Something called CMF. He wouldn't say what it was, but it was going to be fun. It took place in physical therapy rooms, and much to Jim's disappointment, it wasn't co-ed.

Judging from the hootin' and hollerin' from the boys' end, something much greater went on there than the girls' end. All that happened at our end was some stripping off of sweaters, some terry cloth mitts wrung out in ice water and lots of rubbing afterwards with dry towels. Seems this mysterious and fun filled CMF stood only for Cold Mitten Friction, and it was reputed to do wonders for artery polishing. It also felt cold. I opted for a warm shower instead, and rated the title of "chicken."

7:45 A.M.

Breakfast was a big deal, as the feeling was to emphasize breakfast and the midday meal, and de-emphasize the evening dinner. The outside world operates differently, but here in unreality of the Magic Mountain, there was a world attuned solely to concentration on health. Breakfast managed to be tempting even to the confirmed non-breakfast eater. After all, where coffee and a cigarette once sufficed, something interesting must now be substituted for the forbidden smoke.

9:00 A.M.

Tension management class in the parlor, conducted by Jerry, the Deep Breath King. Lots of tension reduction exercise done sitting down. It must have been a very successful class. I fell asleep.

1:00 P.M.

At lunch Alan Rice asked how it was going. Jeanette admitted that she was hanging onto a pack of cigarettes and was unwilling to throw it out for fear she'd panic when she knew there were none left. Alan encouraged her to turn it in, as the others have done. She refused. When she is ready, she will.

2:30 P.M.

Would you believe gym? And I was trying out all the equipment? I hadn't been in a gym since high school.

3:30 P.M.

I was scheduled for physical therapy where they treated me very gently and offered me a variety of circulation motivations, ranging from the electric light cabinet through damp hot blankets to fire-hose showers.

4:45 P.M.

We had another lecture in the parlor of which I guessed to be either on the benefits of exercise or on the benefits of a good diet. Maybe both, I was right.

6:00 P.M.

It was dinnertime and I wondered where the day had gone. I felt like I'd done nothing and yet, I hadn't been bored or pressured for a moment. I hadn't really had a moment in which to miss, I mean truly miss, that cigarette. I mentioned this to some of the others, "You know," said John, "when I tried quitting by myself, I spent so much time being mad at the world. Here I am not mad at anyone."

And that, of course was one of the secrets of this Magic Mountain. There was nothing and no one to get mad at. Everyone here cared. Maybe that is the mysterious plus factor.

Their caring had a way of spreading even to me, the outsider. And I found that I started to care, too. It really seemed to matter to everyone that I succeed in what I came for.

I was into the second day of the five-day program. Yesterday, my first day, seemed so long ago. Everyone who happened to mention yesterday inadvertently said, "last Sunday," before realizing that it was only yesterday.

Tuesday, Wednesday, and Thursday wheeled past, all in the same gentle, unchanging, non-pressuring way that was, oddly enough, never dull. I drank my juice and water. I hiked the early morning woods. I listened to lectures on cholesterol and diet and on cancer and smoking.

I gasped at the statistics turned in by our own group. Of the nine enrolled, we'd smoked a sum total of 267 years, an average of one and a half packs a day, at a conservative estimate cost of .40 cents to .60 cents a day, $4.20 per person per week, $218.40 per person per year. Averaging 29 years 9 months of smoking for the group. This came to a cost per person of $6,442.80. For the total of 267 years of smoking for this group of nine people, the cost came to around $58,000. All went, quite literally, up in smoke.

We grew friendly in a very strange way and in a very short time with strangers whom we'd probably never see again. We laughed at Flanagan with her droopy uniform and her marvelous grin as she streaked past us jogging up the hill, twice our age and twice our speed. Sometimes, she even ran backwards!

We kidded Jerry about his preoccupation with shining up our arteries; with Alan Rice and his interest in our cardiovascular systems. We listened to the dietitian's lecture on how to prepare rather lovely meals from the most unbelievable of raw materials.

We learned to live with and care about, if only on this short term basis, a mortician, an auto-body repairman, a real estate developer, and an ex-Navy career man. Our group was pretty average in all ways.

And then all at once, it was Friday morning. Graduation, speeches, and congratulations commenced. A decision card was given to each of us which read as follows: *Because I believe tobacco is detrimental to my health and illness due to smoking would both jeopardize the security of those I love and hinder further ser-*

vice to the community, I hereby choose to cease smoking from this day forward.

It was up to me to sign it or not. And only up to me to know if I had signed it. Then my name was called. I got the giggles. I felt silly and teary at the same time. I desperately wanted a cigarette. I took a deep breath and remembered that I could choose not to smoke for a mere thirty seconds. I stood up to take my certificate of achievement. I read it with a sense of pride that chased away the giggles. The doctor in charge of the program and the program coordinator signed it. My name was centered prominently in firm lettering.

"Because," it read, "you have taken as your motto 'I CHOOSE NOT TO SMOKE' and do not smoke, because you have thus shown your intention to care for your life and the lives of others both by precept and example, adults and children alike, this certificate is given. It may be proudly exhibited." I was now a non-smoker.

Chapter
20

WALLA WALLA AND BEYOND

We spent the next eight years in Walla Walla, Washington. Ruby had major surgery in January 1980, seven months after relocating. She recovered well and began working for a local Home Health agency. By this time Mark had decided to join us. He enrolled in a two-year Respiratory Therapy program at Walla Walla Community College. Graduating in 1986, he left for the University Hospital in Kansas City, where he had been hired. Tim, meanwhile, was enrolled at Pacific Union College and graduated in June of 1988 with a Bachelor of Arts degree in psychology. He later moved to San Diego.

My work at Walla Walla General Hospital, in addition to the normal bedside duties, included initiating a Grief Recovery Program that was offered four times a year and co-sponsored by Community Hospice. Theology students from Walla Walla College were given hands-on experience in bedside ministry, encouraged by two very supportive teachers, Henry Lamberton and Larry Vaverka. Clergy education featured various medical specialists who addressed groups of community pastors in the hospital's auditorium. An employee singing group, with a guitarist, was organized and walked the hallways at mid-morning, sometimes accompanied by Tom Werner, then administrator. Patients loved it.

One day an elderly patient, very hard of hearing, and unresponsive, was surrounded by family members who knew that the end was near. Then the singing group passed by, the familiar words of "Marching to Zion" on their lips. Suddenly the patient sat up straight and said in words everyone could hear: "Wonderful, wonderful." When the group had passed, she fell back and died shortly thereafter. Members of the family told me that the singing group helped their loved one to die in peace. "We will never forget that day as long as we live. Your hospital is so different. The atmosphere is so full of love. Please keep on singing."

Heeding the council of E.G. White in *Testimonies* Vol. 6 p. 78, we also organized a Clergy Support Group. She had written, "Our ministers should seek to come near to the ministers of other denominations. Pray for and with these men...manifest a deep and earnest interest in these shepherds of the flock." Representatives of four denominations met monthly in the hospital chapel, sharing and praying together. They, not I, decided to fine latecomers to these meetings by charging $1.00 for every minute they were tardy. During the years that followed no fines were issued.

While working at Walla Walla General Hospital, an incident occurred that impressed me deeply. It taught me how important it is not to leave home without settling arguments with our loved ones.

One morning the Emergency Department called me to comfort a young mother whose husband had just been pronounced dead. While working in the woods a falling tree had crushed him. As the wife approached the emergency entrance where a nurse and I waited, she sensed something ominous and shouted, "Is he gone?"

When the nurse confirmed her suspicion, she let out the most agonizing cry I had ever heard.

"No! No! It can't be! Tell me it isn't so! We had an argument last night and didn't make up before he left for work."

Once inside she threw herself upon the lifeless body of her husband, pounding his chest with clenched fists, screaming one minute and pleading the next.

"I didn't mean it! I'm so sorry! Wake up! I need you! The baby needs you! Oh, oh,...please, doctor, help him! Do something! Anything to bring him back!"

It took us the better part of an hour to calm her down so she could drive herself home. When I inquired regarding her church affiliation and the name of her pastor, there was no response. Religion had not been part of their lives.

Similar tragedies are not uncommon, perhaps not as traumatic. In my work I have discovered that many people fail to consider the consequences of unresolved conflicts. Expensive caskets and elaborate funerals can never take the place of reconciliation and forgiveness.

Also, at this time we experienced God's intervention in a dramatic way during a trip to Canada in the winter of 1986.

Ruby and I, accompanied by her cousin Virginia Fleck, had attended a Alumni Homecoming at Canadian Union College that November. Our trip to Lacombe had been uneventful, and our Honda Accord, equipped with snow tires, had performed well. We anticipated no problems on our way home.

Driving on Highway 95 between Radium Hot Springs and Cranbrook in British Columbia late in the evening, we encountered snow. The farther south we drove, the harder it snowed, making the roads slick, and limiting visibility. Several vehicles had passed us going in the opposite direction, creating temporary blind spots of swirling snow as they sped by.

Suddenly I noticed headlights in my rear-view mirror. A vehicle was gaining on us rapidly and obviously intent on passing. I slowed down. A pick-up truck pulled ahead, throwing a thick cloud of snow into our path, which caused me to lose sight of the road. Taking my foot completely off the gas, I hoped to slow down gradually while finding my way through the snow flurries. Instead, our car went into a skid, turned completely around and came to rest in a deep snow bank on the east side of the highway. Fortunately, the front end pointed toward the road.

Hitting the snow bank, Virginia, who had been sitting in the back seat, was thrown against the right rear door, breaking out the entire window. A blast of icy air entered the car. She suffered some minor bruises but Ruby and I were not hurt. The snow bank had cushioned us. We breathed a sigh of relief and sent up a prayer of thanks to our Lord, at the same time asking Him to send us help.

After several failed attempts to move the car forward the engine quit. When I tried getting out, my door would not open against several feet of packed snow. Finally, I crawled out through the window. By then another pick-up truck approached and stopped. The driver connected a chain and pulled us back on the road. When I tried to start the engine again, nothing happened. The other driver also tried, without success.

"It looks like you will need a mechanic," he said. "I'll have to go on. Hope someone with better skills then mine will come along soon." With that he was off.

Now what? It was past 9 p.m. and still snowing. With the right rear window gone, it was uncomfortably cold inside the car. I prayed, "Lord, please send us someone who knows something about fixing engines." Minutes after I finished my prayer another car slowed down and stopped. It was heading South, the same direction we were traveling. The driver came over to investigate.

"Having problems?" he asked.

"Sure do. Can't get my engine going and I'm not a mechanic!"

"You're lucky," he grinned, "I am." Walking briskly to the car, he asked to take a look.

He got into the driver's seat and fumbled with the ignition key. *Is he really a mechanic?*, I thought to myself. Opening the hood he worked briefly underneath. Soon the engine was running. While I stared in disbelief as he closed the hood, this friendly stranger smiled broadly and asked, "Where are you people from, and where are you heading?"

"We are headed for Walla Walla, Washington," I replied, "We just came from Lacombe."

"Lacombe, eh?" Smiling still, "That's were we just came from."

"What a surprise, so you know the area?" Pointing to the back seat, I said, "this is my wife's cousin, Virginia. She visited her parents who live in Lacombe, while my wife and I attended an Alumni Homecoming at the college just north of town."

An even wider grin now played around his lips as he said, "We were at that Homecoming too!"

"Then you are Adventists?" I asked with excitement.

"Yes! Both my wife and I graduated from Canadian Union College."

"Praise the Lord!" I half shouted. "To think He sent you to help us." *I had no idea how far we were from the next service station and didn't look forward to spending the night on the road, stuck like this.* "So God sent us not just any mechanic, but a fellow believer! Wait till the ladies hear this."

After sharing this news with Ruby and Virginia, they rejoiced with me.

"My name is Jake Fortney," he said. "You ladies are welcome to ride with my wife in the station wagon." Then turning to me, "Let me take a look at your rear axle. You must have hit the bank pretty hard. I may need your help."

He crawled under the rear of my car and looking carefully, announced, "Your axle is bent and the right rear tire is out of alignment. I'll have to pull it back a bit."

He walked over to his car and got a chain, connected it to my rear axle and then backed his vehicle until the chain could be attached to his back bumper.

"I need you to get in your car and keep your foot on the brake while I pull forward." In several short spurts, he tugged at the axle until he was sure it was straight enough for driving. "You'll be able to drive now," he said. "But not fast. I'll drive your car to Cranbrook. You join the ladies in my car and follow me. We have about 40 miles to go."

It took another hour to get to Cranbrook where we found a motel and stayed the night. During the trip we learned from Mrs. Fortney that her husband had worked as an automobile mechanic for several years before accepting his present teaching position in the Adventist grade school at Creston B.C.. On their way back from Lacombe, they had stopped in Radium Hot Springs to relax in the warm pool.

"We lingered a lot longer in that nice hot water than we had intended. God must have directed that delay or we would've missed you," Mrs. Fortney reminded us.

"It is nothing short of a miracle that you came along when you did," I added. "Being stuck in the middle of nowhere with no mechanical skills, the outlook was bleak."

"God answers prayer in mysterious ways sometimes, doesn't He?" Mrs. Fortney whispered softly.

Deeply moved, Ruby agreed: "It was an *instant* answer to prayer."

The Fortneys stayed with us until we were settled in the motel. When I offered to pay them something for their trouble, Jake refused, saying: "Pass the favor on to someone else in need."

The next morning we got some help from the local Honda dealer in sealing the back window temporarily, assuring us a comfortable interior while we crawled back to Walla Walla, not exceeding 35 miles per hour. We arrived home late that evening, but were glad to be safe and sound, thanks to God who sent a mechanic just in time.

Chapter
21

WE MOVE AGAIN

In the summer of 1987, we responded to an invitation from Kurt Ganter, administrator at Parkview Hospital in Brunswick, Maine, to direct their chaplaincy program. I enjoyed almost two years in that facility until Kurt transferred. During that time Ruby worked in a nursing home as Assistant Director of Nurses. Kurt's successor had someone else in mind for my position, so we transferred to Hackettstown, New Jersey. Gene Milton, CEO of Hackettstown Regional Medical Center, welcomed me cordially and gave me his full support during the next five years. Again we initiated a grief recovery ministry, an employee-singing group, and community clergy education. Ruby found employment with a Home Health agency of the State of New Jersey.

During my fourth year at Hackettstown, the local United Methodist Church invited members of our administration and all department heads to an Appreciation Celebration. It was to be a part of their regular

Sunday morning service.

The spacious sanctuary was filled to capacity. On the platform were the senior pastor and two of his associates. One, Mark Odenwelder, was in semi-retirement but still active, visiting parishioners in nursing homes and hospitals. He often ate in the hospital cafeteria and periodically requested my assistance. We became good friends.

That morning he announced the opening hymn and read from the Scriptures prior to the pastoral prayer by the other Associate. Following the choral presentation, the senior pastor stood up and began his sermon. Suddenly there was a quick movement behind the rostrum. Mark had fallen from his chair and lay sprawling on the platform floor. Audible gasps could be heard from all sections of the sanctuary. Everyone strained to watch the unfolding drama. Several nurses and one of our physicians rushed to Mark's side and began CPR. They took him to a back room while the congregation prayed and sang hymns. Half an hour later the senior pastor received a hand-written note and announced to the congregation, "It appears as though the Reverend Odenwelder suffered a massive heart attack and does not respond to CPR. Due to this tragedy, the service is now concluded. Appreciation Day will have to be postponed."

Three months later Otto Froehlich, a hospital volunteer and member of our employee-singing group, also met a sudden death. Gifted with a strong voice despite his 84 years, he had joined the group two years previously. He couldn't always be with us due to scheduling conflicts, but he came when he could.

One morning, while we descended the cement stairway from the fourth to third floor, he lost his balance, fell and was knocked unconscious. Despite the

best efforts by the medical staff, he never regained consciousness and died a week later.

Otto wasn't much of a churchgoer, but he believed
in prayer. In fact, that very morning he had entered
the chapel ahead of everybody else. This was unusual,
for he was generally the last one to show up due to a
leg injury that caused him to limp. He sat there alone,
head bowed, praying. Did he have a premonition? We
will never know this side of heaven.

Both of these men died while in active service for
Christ. Otto Froehlich's faithfulness was honored by
naming the recently added Emergency Pavillion of the
medical center after him.

To most of us, death doesn't come as quickly and
painlessly. Whenever I think of the passing of these
two men I am reminded of a 69-year-old patient suffering from severe pulmonary emphysema, a condition
that causes shortness of breath, anxiety, and depres-
sion. This visit took place in St. Helena, in their In-
tensive Care Unit, where Henry (not his real name)
had been admitted and re-admitted over a three-year
period. We were well acquainted. Because he was on
oxygen, he spoke only in short sentences. As I sat next
to his bed one evening he grabbed my arm and blurted
out: "Chaplain, what's it like to die?"

We had gone over the Bible teaching about death
many times before. (John 11:11, Dan. 12:2; 1 Thess.
4:15–18) These texts describe death as simply a sleep.
Apparently, Henry needed to hear them again, so I
obliged as he looked intensely into my face and held
tightly unto my arm. Finally, he ordered, "Pray with me
and go on home. I'm not afriad to die anymore." Com-
mitting him to the care of our loving heavenly Father,
I left, saying: "Remember, Henry, when it happens it'll
be like going to sleep, and the next thing you'll see is

the face of Jesus." He smiled and waved good-bye.

Shortly after arriving home the telephone rang. It was the ICU supervisor. "I've just got to tell you this," she almost shouted, "the nurse assigned to Henry looked in on him shortly after you left. He was resting peacefully and told her: "I'm going to sleep now." Thinking that he wanted to be left alone, she went about her business. When ten minutes later she again checked on him, he was gone...with a beautiful smile on his face."

Epilogue

In the early part of 1993, during a routine examination by my internist, a heart irregularity was noticed, indicating one or more occluded coronary arteries. He recommended open-heart surgery. Instead, I opted to go to the Weimar Institute in northern California. Ruby and I spent 19 days there, learning a new lifestyle that was implemented immediately. Despite a strict vegan diet and daily exercise, it became evident by the end of that summer that stress was the predominant cause of my condition. Retirement seemed to be the most promising solution. I was 63 years old at the time.

We returned to Walla Walla in September where our home, having been rented, was waiting for us. Ruby worked for five more years as a home health nurse. Meanwhile, I discovered the blessings of volunteer service that I can perform at my own pace and keep stress to a minimum. There have been church-sponsored trips to Alaska, Arizona, and Rosario Beach on the Washington coast, to assist with building and renovation projects. Most of my volunteer time is spent at Walla Walla General Hospital where I feel at home, *escorting* patients and visitors. On rare occasions I get to be chaplain again.

Our sons, meanwhile, are pursuing their professions. Mark has married a phlebotomist and works as a respiratory therapist in Reno, Nevada. Tim, now living on the island of Bali, Indonesia, enjoys surfing and being a bachelor while earning his living as a photojournalist. We pray for them daily.

Hans and Malchen Zuber now rest, awaiting the coming of Jesus. Malchen lived several years longer than her husband despite the severe trauma she experienced in her kitchen.

In November 2000, Ruby was diagnosed with a non-Hodgkins lymphoma. She took her prescribed number of chemotherapy treatments and is now in remission. For 15 years we had been part of a small prayer group that met every Tuesday morning. We both believe that her recovery is due mostly to those prayers, although we watch our diets and exercise regularly. In May 2005, I finally had quadruple bypass surgery but recovered rapidly. On June 16, 2008, Ruby and I gratefully celebrated our 50th wedding anniversary. To God be the glory.

While we do not know what the future holds, we trust Him who directs it. We believe His promise in Hebrews 13:5, "I will never leave you nor forsake you."

Postscript

During 28 years of chaplaincy, I have come to appreciate the wise counsel contained in the book, *Ministry of Healing*, by Ellen White. The following quotations from that book have been helpful to me.

"Those who surrender their lives to His guidance and to His service will never be placed in a position for which He has not made provision." (p. 248)

"Nothing tends to promote health of body and soul than does a spirit of gratitude and praise. It is a positive duty to resist melancholy, discontented thoughts and feelings – as much a duty as it is to pray. If we are heaven-bound, how can we go as a band of mourners, groaning and complaining all along the way to our Father's House?" (p. 251)

"The consciousness of right-doing is one of the best medicines for diseased bodies and minds. When the mind is free and happy from a sense of duty well done and the satisfaction of giving happiness to others, the cheering, uplifting influence brings new life to the whole being!" (p. 257)

"Often your mind may be clouded because of pain. Then do not try to think. You know that Jesus loves you. He understands your weakness. You may do His will by simply resting in His arms." (p. 251)

We invite you to view the complete
selection of titles we publish at:

www.LNFBooks.com

or write or email us your praises,
reactions, or thoughts about this
or any other book we publish at:

TEACH Services, Inc.
P.O. Box 954
Ringgold, GA 30736

info@TEACHServices.com

www.ingramcontent.com/pod-product-compliance
Lightning Source LLC
Chambersburg PA
CBHW060543100426
42742CB00013B/2432